RICH£R
ON LEADERSHIP

By Julian Richer

with Kate Miller

Published by Richer Publishing
Richer House, Hankey Place,
London SE1 4BB

First edition published 1999 © Julian Richer 1999

Further copies of "*Richer on Leadership*" are obtainable from bookshops or
direct from the publisher on tel: 0171 378 9730 or fax: 0171 378 9744.

ISBN 0 9534415 0 4
Printed and bound in Great Britain by
Saffron Reprographics

Julian has substantial interests in many businesses including "Richer Sounds" the U.K's biggest hi-fi retailer, having opened his first shop at the age of 19, which holds the record for the highest sales per square foot of any retail outlet in the world.

His interests cover manufacturing, retail, leisure, distribution, recruitment, publishing, consultancy and property.

Although not keen on public speaking, he was made the youngest ever "Business Communicator of the year" for 1996.

He now spends more time on his philanthropic interests, which include free consultancy work for the heads of some of the U.K's largest charities and a Foundation which helped 250 good causes last year. He is also a director of Duchy Originals (the Prince of Wales' charitable trading company) and also one of only eight official "Ambassadors for Youth".

In addition, he is a member of the Board of the Management & Enterprise Training Organisation and he chairs the independent evaluation panel of the Irwell Valley Housing Association, is acting Chair for both the National Appeal Committee for the R.N.I.B., and the Amnesty International Appeal Leadership Group as well as a panelist for the Department of Trade & Industry's 'Consumers' First' Award Scheme.

He is the youngest Governor of Clifton College, his old school and this is in spite of his poor performance there.

One of his companies "Richer Consulting" advises some of the country's largest organisations at chief executive level on staff motivation, customer service, cultural change, communications and suggestion schemes and his book "The Richer Way" was the best selling business book at WH Smith when it was published in November 1995.

To Rosie

Acknowledgements

My biggest debt goes to Kate Miller who wrote this book with me: my thoughts and her hard work to be precise.

Thanks to various colleagues who worked through the proofs and gave their valuable input: Teresa, my diary secretary, David Robinson my Group Managing Director, James Johnson-Flint, John Dalton and Richard Squibb, my distributor.

My friend and adviser Richard Pennycook spent a lot of time and effort giving me the benefit of his considerable wisdom regarding the structure of the book, not all of which I was able to incorporate into this first edition, but nonetheless "thank you".

Claudia, my Group Marketing Director who spent a lot of time getting printing quotes and her colleagues who designed the book cover so a huge "thank you" to them.

In addition, I would like to extend my thanks to Francis Loney who, once again, has used his magical photographic powers to make me look almost human (!) and, last but not least a big "thank you" to Chrissie, my P.A. for bringing the whole project together.

Contents

Introduction

After my first book, "The Richer Way" was published I felt it might be useful to write a more specific guide relating to my experiences of running businesses. Having been a business founder, leader and manager for over 20 years I thought there must be some tips and guidance I could give others on the subject, if only to help them prevent making some of the same silly mistakes I had made.

This isn't a definitive guide but one based upon my own experiences of the businesses I've been involved with. Indeed, as I get older and hopefully wiser, I am sure there will be more I will be able to add to this first manuscript.

Leadership can actually be a lonely affair. I hope this book will give you some support.

Julian Richer

September, 1998

Chapter I

Leading from the front

The biggest failure that I see in organisations today is failure of leadership.

My first book, "The Richer Way", was about the importance of focusing on people. The primary measure of any organisation's success is customer satisfaction. To achieve that satisfaction, employers must focus on their company's most important asset – its people – because it is only well-motivated and well-managed staff who give customers an excellent service.

That book has sold more than 30,000 copies, so somebody out there must think my message is a useful one. Very many businesses and services are recognising the paramount importance of motivating their staff and giving good customer service. Yet many are also falling short in their efforts to achieve this. The reasons, in my observation, are nearly always due to failures at the top.

I believe you learn most about an organisation from talking to its staff. That is why, in my own company, we make sure feedback from the workforce is constantly being passed up to me and my senior managers. When I visit other businesses, I try to make a point of talking to staff and junior managers and this invariably gives me an insight into the state of the business. What I hear frequently is an account of weak leadership – lack of decision making, chiefs with poor credibility because they say one thing and do another, bosses hiding behind their managers when times are tough. That company's profits may look good on paper, but its performance is poor. Weak leadership creates a disgruntled and resentful workforce and, sooner or later, service to the customer will suffer.

The bookstalls are full of management books expounding the latest theory. But management is not enough - successful organisations need leadership.

This is the huge difference between the leader and everyone else in the organisation. Everyone else does their job and can contribute to the organisation's development. But the leader has the definitive imprint on the organisation. That sounds obvious, yet many chiefs fail to address the responsibilities that places on them. I thrive on the responsibility. Some people might be afraid of it and never want to be a leader. Others think they want that power but do not live up to its demands.

There is no escaping the fact that the leader's decisions make the difference between good and bad performance. Of course there are outside factors, like the state of the economy. But even in recessions there are winners and losers. Whether a business is a winner or a loser depends on the quality of it's leader's strategy, and his or her ability to motivate people and drive the business forward.

Admittedly, a company with a monopoly should succeed whether the leader is good or bad. Other companies with good leaders may still fail. But on the whole, the performance of a business is down to its leader. In particular, a good leader makes all the difference in the long term between average performance - which in reality usually means falling behind the market - and great performance.

So there can be huge value added by the leader. This should be tested in reality. When I become involved with a business, whether as a consultant, a non-executive director or as chairman, I ask not to be paid, but to have a share of the value I add, whether that is profits or share price. So I put my money where my mouth is. I would argue more business people should go in as chair on this basis, particularly if they are successful people already earning plenty. Their rewards should be linked solely to the performance of the company. Willingness to do this is a mark of good leadership.

So what makes a leader? It is not the size of the company. A good leader might be at the head of a workforce of two or of 200,000. They might be leading a multinational company, their own business which they have started from scratch, a charity, a primary school or a corner shop. Whatever the organisation, without a leader to inspire staff and drive the business forward, it will stagnate and fail.

Are you a leader? Try this simple test. Your company is heading £200,000 into the red. Do you:

a)   sack 20 people?

b)   cut your own salary?

c)   sell the Rolls Royce and switch off the fountain in the head office lobby?

If your answer is a) before b) or c), you are definitely not a leader. If you reluctantly decided c), you are on the right lines, but have you wondered how you got into the red in the first place?

The point is that leadership is not about what you can get other people to do, it is about what you do yourself.

It is not necessarily the cleverest people who make good leaders. It is the ones who can get their message over to others. To be a good leader you must be able to inspire people.

A good leader has a story to tell – a story about how everyone is going to pull together and succeed. To be a strong leader you must believe in this story, and you must also shout it loud. You have to make sure all the people working for you know the story and that everything you do personally and that the organisation does as a whole, fits in with the plot. If your actions are not in keeping with your words, the story will soon lose its magic.

There is not one single successful leadership style. Leaders come in different shapes and sizes, some loud, some quiet, some high profile and others low profile. They will also have arrived at the top job by very different routes. Some people climb the corporate ladder until they reach the top. Others are entrepreneurs like myself who head a business they created themselves. Neither of these routes automatically makes you a leader. Some people do well in the corporate world because they know how to play by the rules: when they are appointed to head a company and find that there is no-one to tell them what to do and they have to write their own rules, they flounder. These are usually the chiefs who lack vision and are terminally indecisive.

Entrepreneurs tend to be highly enthusiastic about their own business. But some find it very difficult to make the leap from, say, one shop which they run, to a chain of shops which they have to lead. Unless they can learn to let go and to focus on their staff, they too can be poor leaders, autocratic and interfering.

Entrepreneurial people like myself have advantages and disadvantages. The advantages are that we identify closely with our business and drive it energetically. The downside is that the moment we take our foot off the pedal, the business slows down. Everyone is looking to us for leadership.

This is a problem. Although I've said the leader makes a big difference to the performance of an organisation, that business will be weak if there is only one person making the engine turn over. Another mark of good leadership is that the organisation should flourish even when he or she is not there. To create a business with real longevity and staying power in the organisation, it must not be reliant on one person, a kind of corporate extension of the leader.

This is a difficult balance for entrepreneurs to strike and I have worked hard to achieve it in my companies. I want them to thrive without me, so that, say, if ever I want to sell, they have a value without me. The danger is that something will be lost without my drive and experience. So I try to harness the energy of the whole board, so it is not reliant on my energy.

One of the steps we've taken, for example, is to set up a management board at Richer Sounds. Previously we had only the group board for my whole group of 11 companies. The Richer Sounds directors now meet – without me – on a Monday afternoon. Together, they have a lot of enthusiasm and ideas which can power the business. They copy me their minutes after each meeting so I can keep an eye on what is happening.

This book will start by looking at the qualities and skills needed by leaders. While skills and experience are important, it is personal qualities more than anything that mark out a leader from a manager.

By personal qualities I mean the things that have to come from you. As leader, you must have your own vision for your organisation – you cannot hire a consultant or appoint a committee to devise one for you. Determination and drive to succeed also have to come from you. If you have that drive, there's a good chance you can lead your business through even the worst disasters, when everyone else in the organisation has given up. The success of a company often rests on the determination of one person at the top.

The 12 key qualities of a leader are:

1.   Vision. Your vision of what you want your organisation to achieve.
2.   Communication. Your ability to communicate that vision to other people, to inspire and motivate them.
3.   Determination. The single-mindedness that enables you to overcome setbacks and failures.
4.   Restlessness. Good leaders are never complacent. They are always pushing the organisation forward, asking questions, searching for

improvements. Leaders should never be too big to pay attention to detail.

5. Ruthlessness. Ruthless about maintaining standards within the organisation and ruthless about beating the competition.

6. Ability to delegate. You cannot lead unless you know how and when to let go.

7. Independence of mind. A leader should not seek to be liked, but to be respected.

8. Integrity and fairness. This will gain you credibility inside and outside your organisation.

9. Accessibility. The willingness to listen to employees, suppliers and customers, and not to hide behind your managers.

10. Decisiveness. The more you make decisions, the easier it gets. You need to make decisions and own them.

11. Bravery under pressure. The buck stops with you.

12. Ability to learn from experience. A successful business seeks continuous improvement – or kai zen, in the Japanese term. Leaders too should always be developing and improving what they do, seeking fresh ideas and better ways of doing their job.

Few of us are born with all these qualities. But good leaders can learn and develop them. Together, these qualities will generate a particular culture. An organisation that has a culture of innovation, decisiveness and integrity is well on the way to success.

I often talk about the culture of a business and it is very important. Culture is the way people feel about the organisation they work for. The leader has an enormous influence over that culture. To establish a culture of honesty and fairness, the leader must take the first steps.

When leaders join an organisation or get promoted, they inherit a culture. They must then decide whether and how they want to change it. A culture cannot be changed overnight as it is the cumulative product of hundreds of decisions, but the leader's decisions will form the culture.

Good leaders are constantly learning from experience. No-one can know everything when they start out. But you can learn from other people's experience and I have written this book in the hope that some readers can learn from my experience.

If you have read my first book, there may be points in this one which sound familiar, but it does no harm to repeat important principles. This book should complement, not replace, "The Richer Way" and what I have to say about leadership should reinforce the message of my first book. I don't change my story with every book (unlike some famous management consultants).

While I am offering my experience, the best teachers of all are probably your own mistakes. One of the hallmarks of leaders is not that they never make mistakes, but that they have the capacity to learn from them. I have never hidden the fact that I have made errors in my business career. My company has been on the brink of disaster twice, and although I now have a group of thriving and diverse companies, along the way there have been other attempts to start new businesses which failed. If you are constantly trying new things and taking risks, you are bound to have failures. But, with the right leadership skills, you can ensure that the disasters are not terminal and that, in the long run, they are outweighed by the successes.

But why repeat unnecessarily the mistakes others have made? I read many history books and biographies, in the hope that I can learn some secrets of others' success and also learn about their failures. That way, I aim to save myself some time and grief by not falling into the same traps.

The point of this book is that there are short cuts to becoming a strong leader. There is a lot for leaders to learn, but who is there to teach you? If you are lucky, you may have had a good mentor during your career.

But many leaders, especially those who have built up their business themselves, have had to learn as they go along. It is trial and error. This book might save you a few trials by telling you what I have learnt from my errors. Unlike many authors of management books, I have been a leader for 20 years, so why not benefit from my experience?

When I act as a consultant to large companies, I do not advise them to copy what I do. No-one will run their organisation in exactly the way I run mine. But in this book I will set out what I see as the fundamental principles of good leadership.

I also explain some practical strategies for the day to day leadership of the business. The leadership qualities listed above - vision, determination and so on - are no good if they are not communicated effectively to others. You can make swift and brilliant decisions, but if there is no mechanism for ensuring they are implemented throughout the company, you are wasting your time.

I see leaders as people who have the ability to inspire others. But not all charismatic people are leaders, though they might temporarily fool you into thinking they are. Too many employees have experience of a boss who makes a rousing speech after the Christmas dinner every year, but is incapable of devising a firm strategy for the business. Employees quickly see through leaders who are all talk. They may feel motivated for a while, but as soon as they see that the boss can never make a decision and good ideas are never put into practice, they become disillusioned and cynical.

Leadership qualities are worthless unless they can be translated into action to benefit the business. The test of a good leader is, ultimately, whether they can make their organisation perform well.

What exactly is the leader's job? The details will vary widely, depending on what kind of business you are in. But there are certain core tasks which belong to the leader.

Deciding strategy

The leader decides in which direction the organisation is going. He or she must have a vision for the organisation, which defines it, sets it apart from the competition and gives it a mission. The leader must also head the process of devising the strategy – how the organisation is going to achieve its goals. They must always be gathering ideas, looking at the market and the world in which the business operates, thinking one step ahead.

Motivating people

It is people who put ideas into practice, but it is not the leader's job to manage every person in the company. Instead you work via layers of 10. You motivate and develop your 10 senior managers and closest assistants, they then each manage 10 people and the strategy is cascaded down the organisation. If you're a strong leader, you will be able to inspire people to believe in your vision. Your 10 people immediately below you will carry your ideas on to the 10 people they manage. With only four layers you can be leading 10,000 people.

Keeping the control

The leader must have a hand on the tiller because you are the final check to ensure the business does not go on to the rocks. However good your finance directors and accountants, the leader should be watching the figures. You must set up systems so that you have key information feeding back to you – on the state of the budget, cashflow, sales, customer satisfaction and other essential indicators for your business.

Making decisions

When you are the leader, the buck stops with you. You are the ultimate decision-maker in the organisation and it will fall to you to solve the toughest problems.

Driving the business forward

The leader has to be the power source for the business. Your energy, enthusiasm and determination will keep the organisation moving forward when others are flagging. You will ensure that the business is reaching for its goals, not only by motivating people but also by constant monitoring of performance. The leader is a coach for the team – you don't have to do all the work yourself, but you train, inspire and push others to do it and to do it better.

A figurehead for staff

Being the leader should never mean that you are too lofty to be concerned with your people. On the contrary you should be there for your workforce, ready to listen to their views and to be the one they can ultimately turn to if they have a problem. You have to do this as well as say it – so that if a member of staff wants to see you, you find a space in your diary within a few days, not six weeks later. It also means setting up proper systems of communication, like a suggestion scheme that works, and built-in safety valves, so that you get to hear about staff concerns before they mount up into a real problem.

A figurehead for customers and suppliers

It is the leader's job to be the public face of your organisation. You don't have to appear in the media every week, but your customers and suppliers should know your name and how to contact you if they have a problem. You should be their guarantee of quality and if they are unhappy, you must hear about it.

Being the social conscience of your organisation

You should set the ethical standards of your company, and ensure that people keep to them. The leader has huge personal influence over the people in the organisation and you should use this influence to create a culture of integrity.

These key tasks are a combination of the macro and the micro. The leader must be able to operate on both levels. The leader must take the macro view – see the big strategy, look to the horizon – but must also have a clear eye for the micro. The chiefs that fail are the ones who think big but get tripped up by details they have overlooked, or the ones who have great command of the detail but little idea of where they are going in the bigger picture.

Details are important. Admittedly I'm a bit of a control freak, with lists for everything, but in my experience details are often the difference between success and failure. The leader must never be too big for details. Spotting the small discrepancy in figures, before it snowballs into something much bigger, can make the difference between profit and loss. Managing people well is about details too – remembering, not just a particular member of staff's name but their history with the company and something about their personal circumstances. Again, small things like remembering a manager's birthday could make a big difference to their morale, letting them feel recognised by the boss and part of the team.

But although I'm good on details, I never fail to see the wood for the trees. I always have the larger strategy in mind. To be a good leader you constantly have to achieve the right balance between macro and micro. So much of business is about maintaining the balance between forces that pull you in opposite directions.

There is the balance between giving good customer service and making a profit. Sometimes good service means not making a sale today, because if the customer is pleased, they might return to buy something else tomorrow. You can raise your profits by cutting costs, but if the result is a poorer service for customers, you have not achieved the right balance.

Another balance is between motivation and control for staff. There must be enough fun for people to be enthusiastic and energetic, but tight enough procedures to ensure they are doing the right things.

Finally, there are the parallel demands of giving your customers great service as well as value for money. In my company, we believe that if we concentrated only on price and not on service, customers will simply be "plunder hunters", coming to us when we have bargains on offer, but with no loyalty. By trying to give them great service at the same time as great prices, we will have a hook to attract people into our stores and then the idea is that our service will convert them into becoming loyal and profitable customers.

This book is in two parts: the first six chapters look at the task of being a leader. The top job demands the maximum from you and can place great pressure on you as a person. You will be able to cope with these pressures much better if you understand what is involved in being an effective leader and are prepared for the stresses and strains.

A lot of the stress can be dealt with by effective time management and ruthless delegation. I believe leaders should use all the tricks, tools and short cuts they can to help them do the job and I pass on a few ideas that work well for me.

The second half of the book is about putting it all into practice. This covers the strategies I have developed in order to be an effective leader. Some of these might be ideas you can copy or adapt. The whole book is about being an effective leader: starting from the inside, with the right qualities and approach, then translating this into action so that you are leading a successful organisation.

Being a leader can be daunting and stressful, but it should also be exciting and fulfiling. I believe it can be the best job in the world.

Chapter 2

Taking the lead

Being a leader is like no other job. There can ultimately be only one leader in any organisation and that leader must have an irreplaceable impact on the business and its people. That doesn't mean the organisation goes to pieces when the leader is not there: on the contrary, a successful chief executive will have the systems in place to ensure operations run smoothly and strategy is followed in his or her absence. But the leader must put a unique stamp on the organisation and, in the long run, must take responsibility for its success or failure.

When you are leader, the buck stops with you. Everyone says this, but how many have really thought through and taken on board what it means? If, like me, you have always been your own boss, you probably understand and accept this. But if you have been promoted to the top job or brought in to head up an organisation, it can be a shock to realise that there is no safety net. You can no longer pass the difficult decisions on to someone more senior: there is no-one more senior.

You can have the best board of directors and senior managers in the world, but that does not remove ultimate responsibility from the leader. The board of the Richer Group takes major decisions and I would not be without my board members. But in the end, as I often joke to them, the company is my train set. There's a right way to do things, a wrong way and there's my way - and we do it my way.

That means the leader cannot dodge responsibility for mistakes. There are frequent examples of bosses blaming the workforce, managers, technical breakdowns or the weather for their company's failings. Those bosses have not understood what it means to be a leader.

Leaders lead, which means the rest of the organisation follows – not like sheep but because they know they have a job to do and are motivated to do it. The leader's task is to ensure they are motivated and that the jobs they are doing are the right ones. You might have a crack analytical mind, a charismatic personality, an MBA from Harvard and a bold strategy for the future, but unless your brilliant decisions are being put into effective action by the people in the front line of your organisation, you are failing as a leader.

This is not to say that being a leader is all about making your organisation run like clockwork. Leadership is about much more than good management. There are thousands of managers out there in all types of business and service, and many are very competent. But many are poor leaders. Their staff have no particular loyalty to them and are more often frustrated than motivated by their manager.

Leaders must inspire. This book is principally aimed at people at the head of their organisation, but inspirational people can be found in all walks of life and at all levels of the organisation. There are middle managers who successfully inspire and lead their team. Looking back at our school days, most of us, if we are lucky, can remember teachers who inspired us, or sports coaches or youth leaders. They weren't managers but they brought out the best in us. It is this quality which combines with management skills to create an effective leader.

Inspiration needs to be handled with care, of course. History shows many dictators who were swept to power by their dangerous ability to inspire. But benign leaders need to inspire too. In business – and again, there are also many examples from politics – being good at the job is rarely enough. You have to capture people's imagination to inspire their loyalty.

I aim to inspire, but I don't aim to be liked. I have never set out to be liked as a leader. That is a trap that many people, notably politicians, fall into. Wanting to be liked by everybody, they have no coherent strategy and end up seeming insincere.

Rather than being liked, I would want to be judged as a fair person and an able manager.

The two elements are important. I want to be seen as competent at what I do. Yet if I'm a good manager but act in an unfair way, I could end up a despot. Being seen as a fair person is very important if you are to have the respect of everyone in your organisation. To have credibility across the whole business you must be sure that people have confidence that, if a problem comes up, you will deal with it in a fair way

So leaders shouldn't lose any sleep over whether they are popular. As kids, we were probably not close to the teachers who inspired us and may have known little about them as people, but they still had a huge impact on us. It is that type of leadership we can emulate at work.

An essential part of inspiration is communication. You cannot be an effective leader without being an effective communicator. It is impossible to motivate people without communicating with them, which means not just talking to people but listening to them.

The importance of communication becomes clear when you look at three of the most vital attributes a leader must have: vision, integrity and the willingness to be there for staff, suppliers and customers. These are things the top person must develop personally. There must be no substitute within an organisation for the leader's own vision, integrity and readiness to listen.

But as well as being essential elements in the leader's ideas and character, these must be communicated to the rest of the organisation. The leader has to find ways of translating his or her vision into a mission for the company and integrity into a culture of honesty throughout the business. The leader's willingness to listen will create an environment where people genuinely come first.

You must communicate well to reap the full benefits of your strategy. You could be the most caring employer in the world, but if your staff are not aware of what you do for them, it will do nothing to create good morale.

Vision

People like to get behind a leader who has a vision. You've got to believe in your vision and make others believe in it.

Having a vision means you can see where you are going. If you know where you want your organisation to be going, much of the task falls into place. You can formulate a strategy for getting there and the basis for decision making will become clear. As leader, your job is to have a vision you personally believe in and then communicate that to everyone else in your organisation.

Not everyone who finds themselves at the top has a vision. You may have built up a business making toy cars and have no plans other than to carry on making toy cars, because that's what you do. Or you may have climbed the corporate ladder until you're at the top of Conglomerates plc without really thinking about what you would do with this train set once it was yours. But no organisation will succeed in the long term unless its leader has a vision which makes it special and gives it that competitive edge.

A vision is often most evident in smaller organisations, like innovative shops, restaurants and services which have their customers coming back for more. Many schools these days are a good example and the best heads have a vision for their school which has parents from miles around queuing up to send their offspring there.

To develop – and sustain – a vision for a large and diverse business is more difficult. This is a real test of leadership. There are some outstanding examples, like Archie Norman who turned Asda from a near-bankrupt supermarket chain into a market leader with a strong brand image. Clarity of vision is key – if you know what your business stands for, so will your customers.

To develop the vision, the leader needs to be creative, from a business point of view. I couldn't draw a dog or a horse to save my life but I am creative in terms of the ideas I have for my businesses. Being creative means thinking a little differently from the rest, seeing new ways of doing things that will distinguish your company from the pack. It means seeing the bigger picture, so you plan what your organisation could do, instead of what it has done for the last 20 years. It also means having the imagination to see things from the customers' point of view and understand what they want from you.

So to develop a vision, a leader should be open to new ideas. You must know what's in the market, what are the trends and the technology. I travel a lot and find that very stimulating. I also arrange my working week so I am not stuck in a routine but give myself time out of the office and time to think, despite my hectic schedule.

But ideas are just the starting point. A good leader must have the clarity of vision to turn ideas into goals.

Like many organisations, Richer Sounds encapsulates its vision in a mission statement. Ours is in three parts:

1. To provide second to none service and value for money for our customers
2. To provide ourselves with secure, well paid jobs, working in a stimulating, equal opportunities environment
3. To be profitable to ensure our long term growth and survival

This sounds very simple but it is not merely a statement of the obvious. If your organisation doesn't have a mission statement, set up a working party to draw one up. Inspired by the leader's vision, the mission statement puts that vision into principles to which everyone can sign up.

A vision is useless if it exists solely inside the leader's head. However passionately you believe in your vision, it will have no impact unless you communicate it effectively to the rest of the organisation. You must believe in it yourself, or people will quickly see that it is hollow. But if you do believe in it and are intent on using that vision to power the organisation forward, managers and staff will soon get on board. People want to work for an organisation that is going somewhere, and for a leader who knows where the organisation is going.

So once you have formulated a vision you are committed to, the task is to communicate to your people where the company is heading, why it should go there and how it's going to get there. Getting there can be a long and difficult road of course, but if everyone believes in the vision you are much more likely to succeed.

The Richer Sounds mission statement - the Richer Way - is instilled into staff from the moment they join. It is printed on pocket-sized cards and included in the Welcome Pack they are given on their first day. All new recruits to Richer Sounds go on a three-day Virgin Seminar (a pretty intensive programme, known as 'the sausage machine') where they all hear me talk about the Richer Way, why it is so important and why we take customer service so seriously. The message comes directly from me, reinforced by the rest of their training.

The vision cannot remain something theoretical. The leader must constantly be finding ways of translating it into action. So to meet the first part of our mission statement, Richer Sounds is centred on customer service. Staff are rewarded for good service, rather than for sales. The customer's receipt carries a short questionnaire, rating the quality of the service. Sales staff are rewarded if the customer ticks 'excellent', they get nothing for 'good' and are penalised if the customer found the service 'mediocre' or 'poor'.

This is just one of the many ways at Richer Sounds in which we ensure that we work towards our goals. What gets measured and rewarded gets done. I frequently criticise companies which claim they want to offer good service, but in practice reward staff for turnover or market share. Leaders who reward what they want to achieve will see results and gain credibility with the workforce.

Communication

Communicating the vision is a continuous task and the leader must create opportunities for doing this. It is no good standing up after the Christmas dinner, telling everyone the company is heading for great things in the coming year and then staff not hearing another word from you until the following Christmas.

I communicate with everyone in a number of ways. Personal addresses at seminars are very powerful, but I am too busy to do that all the time. So the trick is to communicate your vision at the times when it will have most impact, such as when someone has just joined the company, or when people are gearing up for a busy period. I spend the whole of December visiting every Richer Sounds shop at least once. That way I can motivate the sales staff just as they go into the vitally important Christmas season.

I'm a great believer in getting the message over in person but I cannot be everywhere, so each month I prepare a video which goes out to all the branches. This is a cheap and easy form of communication: I stand in front of a camera and talk for 20 minutes, telling them how we did the previous month, new developments and any other important messages I want to convey. The branches have to play the video to all staff on a Saturday – and we have a way of checking whether they did so. I have no intention of just talking to myself!

Integrity

Good leaders lead from the front: they don't ask their workforce to do things they wouldn't do themselves.

By integrity I don't mean being a paragon of virtue. What people do outside work is their own business. But within the organisation, there must be a bond of loyalty and trust between colleagues. Dishonesty between colleagues is an attack on the integrity of the organisation.

Double standards are an ugly blemish on too many organisations. Nothing saps morale more quickly than people realising that their bosses are only interested in feathering their own nest.

In my own business we take honesty very seriously. A retail business must do so if it is not to start losing money through staff theft, or 'shrinkage' as we call it. But leaders cannot expect honesty and loyalty from staff if they do not display these qualities themselves.

This is a simple principle that too many chiefs fail to understand. You must not impose cutbacks throughout the organisation and then go out and buy a bigger Bentley for yourself. Even if you take the tube to the office, word will quickly get round about the Bentley and, at best, you will lose credibility in the eyes of staff and, at worst, they will be resentful and unco-operative.

In 1998, for example, the Richer Group entered a period of cost cutting, to get on a sounder financial track. There were no pay rises for staff – but for group board members there were real-terms pay cuts. If there's going to be pain, the workforce should see that the people at the top are prepared to take it first.

At an everyday level too, leaders cannot expect staff to be economical and cost-conscious if they are busy ordering a new jacuzzi for the executive washroom. We have never had leather chairs in the boardroom and the only Bentleys in our company are the ones the staff ride around in, when they are the top-performing branch that month.

I think first class rail tickets are over-priced so I don't travel first class unless I can't get a seat in standard. When I go to seminars with senior managers or other colleagues, we all travel standard together. I enjoy the money I earn, but it is important that my managers and staff never see me wasting money. I then have a right to expect them not to waste my cash.

Richer Sounds shops are small and crowded, because we believe in spending our money on staff and on good value for the customer, rather than on shopfittings. But when I buy a holiday home for the staff, I don't stint on fitting it out attractively and comfortably, making it somewhere I would stay myself. I find that people reciprocate by treating the holiday homes with respect.

There are real dangers when the system works against integrity. A classic case, where the people at the top of a company have different interests from the people below them, is where share options are involved.

I once visited a company which was preparing to float on the stock market. Costs were being hammered and staff were very worried. I felt low morale was harming the business and asked the directors if it was really in the interests of the company to go public. "Of course - we've got a lot of money riding on this in share options", they said. But I asked whether it was strategically right for the business. It appeared the directors had never discussed it in those terms and when they did, they started to have doubts. But it was in their interests to float, because they had been paid with share options and only by going public could they cash them in. There was an inherent conflict of interest between what was advantageous for them and what was advantageous to the company and its workforce.

So if you want your organisation to be founded on integrity, do not create systems that have this in-built conflict of interest. The interests of the business should be identical to the interests of the people. Those at the top of the organisation should not be enriching themselves at the expense of the rest. This is not to say the managing director should earn the same as junior colleagues, but staff should have confidence that everyone is working towards the same goals. The leader must structure the organisation so that if it does well, everyone benefits, and if it hits a bad patch, everyone makes sacrifices - and the better you're paid, the bigger the sacrifice.

If everyone's aims are in line, the leader can send clear messages through the organisation, without these becoming distorted by conflicts of interest.

The leader must demonstrate personal integrity. I have no time for chiefs who hide behind their PR department when things go wrong. That is not leadership.

Integrity is about standing up to the difficult tasks. You can't ask people to be honest and loyal and then not be honest with them. When there are poor results or a major service failure, it's no good getting a spokesperson to fob off the press. It's no good dragging in the head of human resources to make the announcement about large-scale redundancies.

It is the leader's job to take the flak. Ownership of mistakes is very important. When we have had a bad season at Richer Sounds I have stood up in front of colleagues and said, "It's my fault, I'm sorry, I let you down - the buck stops with me". People are used to their bosses taking the credit for things, so they will find it refreshing to hear a boss admit to mistakes.

The same applies in the public arena. If an organisation has made a mistake, covering up or denying responsibility will not make the press and public forget about it. But admitting mistakes will take the sting out of criticism.

The important thing is to follow up ownership of mistakes with swift action. If we've had a bad season at Richer Sounds I do not rest until I have found out why and how we can do better next time.

Bosses would have much more credibility with their staff if they stood up and took responsibility in this way. I rarely see business people who are able to do that. Maybe it is part of business culture that no-one must admit to making mistakes and perhaps if they work for public companies they're worried they will get fired. If so, the culture is wrong. The test should be, not whether you make mistakes from time to time, but whether you sort it out and learn from the mistake.

Accessibility

The leader must be there for staff and managers. Accessibility is linked to integrity: however important you are, you should never be too busy to listen to your staff and customers. Again, it means not hiding behind your managers, secretaries and PR people.

Many people, joining a new organisation, are welcomed on the first day by the managing director who says cheerily, "If ever there's a problem, talk to me. My door's always open". Everyone knows this isn't true. For a start, his door is never open and when you try to make an appointment to see him he's busy for three weeks and then he's off to Japan. Secondly, if you did get through the door to speak to him, you would probably be marked down as a nuisance.

In my company we believe our staff are our greatest asset. Lots of organisations say this but few take any steps to protect that asset and ensure it grows in value. Most of our people will routinely go to their manager with their ideas or concerns, but if they do want to talk to me, I have systems in place to ensure that I am accessible.

All staff have my home number and they know they can call me there. Directors of other companies think I am mad when I say this and when I tell them our training centre is in the garden of my house in Yorkshire. The reality is that people do not abuse that access to me and my privacy is not infringed.

Of course, no chief executive is sitting there in the office waiting for people to knock on the door. As leader, you will have enormous pressures on your time, but it is your job to create a climate of accessibility in your organisation and to create that by example. The key is to do this in a structured way.

In my company we do not have annual assessments for staff. We talk to them after six months in the job to see how they are doing, but after that, it is down to them to ask for 'career counselling'. This means they can request a meeting with a senior person to discuss their career, whether there is a specific problem or whether they want to discuss their future direction.

Their career counselling will often be with their manager, but it does not have to be. After all, their problem might be with that very manager. So they can have a session with any senior person, including me.

It's fine saying I do career counselling, but if people ring my diary secretary only to be told I can't see them for six weeks, I will have zero credibility. They know I'm busy and my diary secretary will tell them so, but I always fit them in as soon as possible, within a few days if I can. Even if it can only be a 10 minute meeting, that person will know I have made time for them.

That is a very powerful message to staff. It is also a powerful message to other managers. This open door policy at the very top of the organisation is crucial: if I can make time to speak to people, then all the other directors and managers should have time to speak to their people. It does not take up a huge chunk of my time and I feel it is important. Any chief who says, "I'd like to do that but I couldn't possibly, I'm far too busy", should think again. If you really want to make time for people there is always a way.

It is the same with 'Management By Walking Around'. Many bosses say they know how important this is - but somehow they never find the time. It comes down to your choice. If you believe MBWA is important you can make it happen, but only by scheduling it in your diary.

All this is hard work, especially as your business grows. I used to be able to spend a day in each branch during the run-up to Christmas. Now I generally have to visit two a day in order to get round them all and it does mean I am living out of a suitcase for a month. But it is worth the effort for the loyalty it inspires in people and the benefits I gain from being in touch with every corner of the business.

Accessibility also provides useful safety valves in the organisation. Downward communication is not usually a problem - it is easy to give orders. But to avoid disasters, you need good upward communications. As leader, you need to be able to be told when things are not going right.

Career counselling is one such safety valve. If a colleague is unhappy, I want to know about it and not find out on the day they leave the company. We have a magazine where staff can sound off, and 'question time' at seminars where myself or my managing director are put in the hot seat and people fire questions at us.

Our most important safety valve is the suggestion scheme, which I explain in detail in Chapter 7. This is a communications tool which is open to everybody and is constantly in use. It is one of the features of the company I take most pride in and I believe strongly that the leader must front the suggestion scheme if it is to work.

I also believe in being accessible to customers - but, again, in a structured way. My picture is in our catalogues and my name is on the customer's receipt, inviting them to tell me if the service was good or bad. This is not an ego trip for me: it is question of responsibility. A company should have one figurehead whom customers can hold responsible and who is powerful enough to sort out problems for them.

However, unlike certain other high profile chiefs, I don't ask customers to "pick up the phone" if they have any comments. It is very unlikely that they will be able to get through to me and they will end up even more dissatisfied. I ask them to write and explain the problem. I then ask the manager or member of staff involved to give their account of the situation. Having heard both sides of the story, I can then give an informed reply to the customer.

I hate bullshit. I hate it when people tell you they will do something and don't do it, and never intended to do it. I hate it when people say "we must have a meeting", but when you ring up their diary is always full, or when bosses invite ideas from staff and then completely ignore them, or when companies invite feedback from customers but take no action as a result. As a consultant, I regularly come across these failings - often in highly-rated companies.

I try to make sure I don't bullshit as a leader by putting in systems to ensure I do what I say I will do. So my vision for the company is not some empty aspiration but goals we work towards. I avoid hypocrisy and double standards and try to make sure that when we say we value staff and customers, we can demonstrate that in practice. Your goals as a leader might be different, but you must approach them with the same integrity if you are to have any credibility and effectiveness. It has to come from you.

Chapter 3

Determination, delegation, decision making

There are three Ds which mark out the successful leader from the rest. A leader has to have fantastic determination, to be a good delegator and a strong decision-maker.

Determination

The biggest factor in success is not brilliance or luck, but determination. Plenty of good leaders are not outstandingly clever. I didn't shine academically at school (I was too busy buying and selling hi-fis) and I don't have an MBA. Good leaders do need a certain amount of street sense, or an instinctive feel for their business. They need a modicum of luck, although, on the whole, you make your own luck. But what they have in abundance is determination.

Luck is often used as an explanation for people's success. But there are two types of luck - passive and active. Passive luck is mainly a matter of birth: being fortunate enough to be able-bodied, intelligent and living in a country where you can be educated and benefit from a relatively free and stable society. Active luck arises from taking opportunities. It may be fortunate that the opportunities come your way but what really matters is whether you make the most of them or not. We should be thankful to have passive luck but active luck we must create ourselves.

The difference between me and other people who start out in business but do not get very far, is not that I'm more able, but that I had the determination to succeed. Often there is no secret to this: it is a matter of getting up when you've been knocked down, trying again and again until you get it right. Whether you're heading your own business or another kind of organisation, you need this tenacity.

It requires self-belief, though not arrogance, which would prevent you learning from your mistakes. As a leader, you are responsible for colleagues who have put their trust in you, so you also owe it to them to maintain that determination. All organisations have successes and failures, but the ability to bounce back is more important than getting it right every time.

When I opened my first Richer Sounds shop on London Bridge Walk we did well for the first year. Business seemed to be booming. I was 21, I bought a sports car and a flat in Regents Park. It all came crashing down and when the true figures emerged months later, an initial £20,000 surplus had turned into a £130,000 loss.

I went to a friend's father, a successful businessman, for advice and showed him the books. I was astonished when he advised me to give up. It had never once occurred to me to close the shop - it was my life.

I was inexperienced, but determined. I brought in new auditors, sold my flat, stopped taking a salary out of the company for a while and managed to drag the business back from the brink.

We went through a second rocky patch a few years later, when we grew too fast. We expanded from four to 16 shops in less than two years and ended up under-capitalised. This time I was more confident that the problems could be solved. We closed five branches and put the company back on the rails.

My two partners in my restaurant business showed themselves to be equally determined. When they opened in 1996, they had real difficulties at first with the most important element in their business - the food. They tried several chefs who proved to be not up to scratch, but they didn't give up. Finally they found an excellent chef. A week later, by coincidence, Evening Standard reviewer Fay Maschler walked in the door and liked her meal so much she went back the same day. If she had visited only a week earlier her review would have been damning and the restaurant would have been in serious trouble. After her review the takings increased five-fold and the restaurant has not looked back.

This was achieved through pure determination. My partners were not satisfied with the cooking, they would not compromise their standards and they persisted until they found the right chef. They had invested all their money in this restaurant and were determined to make it succeed.

Bravery under pressure

People want to look up to a leader who doesn't panic, who can face problems and deal with them.

As I've said, admitting to mistakes is an important part of personal integrity. It also takes bravery. When you're the boss, it is easy to blame everyone else for mistakes – who's going to argue with you? It requires a lot more courage to acknowledge responsibility.

Owning mistakes goes hand in hand with learning from them. You cannot do that if you haven't the courage to face the mistakes and find out exactly what went wrong.

Keeping a cool head in times of difficulty is essential for the leader. People get tired of a chief who gets in a flap over little things. Eventually they hide their mistakes and problems from the boss and that can lead to worse disasters because there's no upwards communication. Dealing with a crisis is the real test of leadership and if you can't cope with the minor problems, you won't convince people of your ability when you hit major ones.

A real leader finds reserves of bravery when under pressure, particularly when it comes to protecting staff. I have seen many times how people, when they take on the mantle of leadership, rise to the task.

This does not only mean protecting your staff's jobs when times are hard. They may need other kinds of protection, for example against bullying or harassment. In my company we take a very hard line on theft and will sack, not only the thief but any colleague who knew about the fraud and colluded in it by not telling us. So that means we must protect absolutely anyone who has the courage to tell us if a colleague is stealing, even if it is only a suspicion. If they have the courage to speak up, we owe it to them to stand by them.

I'm a bit of a wimp physically but I always feel I would fight to the death for my staff. Fortunately we're not in the middle ages and I don't have to to defend their honour in a jousting tournament. Even so, it's surprising what physical reserves you can draw on. I'm always telling staff they need to be fit and when I was with a group of them in Blackpool I encouraged them to come for a run with me in the morning. To my horror, 20 of them turned out, all keen to emulate their chairman. I literally had to take the lead, running along the Blackpool seafront. Only five of us finished and believe me, I made sure I was one of them!

Single-mindedness

The determination to overcome problems calls for single-mindedness. This does not mean being stubborn and inflexible, but rather not losing sight of where the business is going.

Never doing a U turn is not the same as being single-minded. U turns are my middle name – every day I'm reviewing my strategy, reassessing situations and making fresh decisions in response to events. A business has to change and evolve to survive. I am constantly thinking about new products and services, new markets and new ways of doing things. But I am single minded about making my business succeed.

As leader, your day will be full of hassles and problems people bring to you. Single mindedness is what gets you through those hassles without losing sight of your vision and strategy. I often picture myself like a batsman at the crease, waiting for the next ball to be bowled at me. I enjoy the challenge of batting away problems.

Restless and ruthless

I often joke that I'm neurotic. Other people might say I'm a perfectionist, pernickety, or just a pain. But while, on the face of it, the person at the top stands above the organisation's day to day hassles, good leaders share my restless search for perfection.

As leader, you are the ultimate check on what your organisation is doing. Don't ever think you are too big for detail. You should have systems in place to ensure quality, but your determination will mean you are constantly pushing and driving the business yourself.

The leader is the one who will go the extra mile to get the service right. If you settle for, "That's OK, the customer will never notice", everyone else in the organisation will too.

By being neurotic I mean leaving as little to chance as possible. I am notorious for double checking everything. If I check things 50 times, 49 times everything will be fine but there will be always be one occasion where I'm glad I checked. Thoroughness is very important: whenever there is a disaster, somewhere back along the line there was someone who said "we don't need to bother" or "we'll do that later". The leader has to be the ultimate check.

Never stop checking just because everything seems to be going fine. The moment you stop will be the moment things start to go wrong. People will probably complain that you are driving them mad with double checking – but that is good. You are there to drive them mad, goad them into doing the job better, because left to themselves, people settle into the easiest way of working and standards slip.

You should also always have a plan B. Again, it seems neurotic, but never take anything for granted, even if it appears a formality. I always ask "what if"? What if a perfectly worked out scheme goes wrong? Do we have a back-up plan?

Thoroughness can be the difference between profit and loss in business. It can ensure you get to a deal faster than the competition, it can mean the difference between a sale and a customer walking out. It requires small things that call for effort – taking notes wherever you go, chasing people up, ringing them back instead of waiting for them to ring you. I have never lost out by being thorough.

When I visit one of our branches, even if the manager has prepared it perfectly for my visit, I will always spot something, a missing price ticket or a dusty display. A good leader is marked out by an eye for detail, and if you don't have that you are in danger of losing touch with your organisation. If I am nitpicking, my staff will learn to be the same.

So many chief executives are caught out by things they hadn't thought about and didn't check. If you want to be a successful leader, you must have your eyes at your back, watching around you and double checking.

You also have to be ruthless, to ensure your organisation is not accepting second place or second best. Clearly a business must be competitive and it is the leader's determination that will keep its competitive edge. Even if your organisation is not competing in a marketplace, the leader must be ruthless about keeping up standards.

I am ferocious about beating the competition. If we ever look through "What Hi-Fi?" magazine and find a company undercutting Richer Sounds' prices we hold an inquisition about it to find out how they got a better deal from the supplier than us. Richer Sounds is the country's leading hi-fi retailer but we don't sit around congratulating ourselves. We are constantly watching the competition and undercutting them where we can. If your business is number 1 in its field you must beware of complacency: it is often a good ploy to imagine you are number 2 and think about how you would try harder.

This doesn't mean making enemies in your marketplace. I find confrontations achieve little and it is often better to run away and fight another day. In my business it is no good falling out with a supplier who has given a better deal to your competitor, because you will only find the next week they have an even more amazing deal which you want to be sure of getting.

I am also ruthless with staff. This does not contradict my belief that staff are our greatest asset, but reinforces it. If you really believe in the value of your workforce, you must never let that value be diluted by people who are not pulling their weight.

In my business we have plenty of carrots to motivate people, but we also have a big stick. It is not used very often but everyone knows it is there. Without a serious threat of discipline, an organisation will slide into anarchy.

If you are waving the stick around every day it loses its impact. Everyone must understand in what circumstances it will be used and it is the leader who must decide. In my company we value integrity, so lying and theft are instant sacking offences. But sometimes too you have to be ruthless with people who simply don't deliver. In that respect I am much much tougher on senior people than juniors. Senior managers in the organisation have to lead from the front.

Often this means swift demotion. We are quick to promote, quick to demote, because that is a way of giving people a chance to try out a new job without risking their entire career. We will give someone a chance to be a branch manager, but if they are not up to it they will be back on the shop floor with no blame attached.

Sometimes you do have to lose people and that can be very unpleasant, particularly if your business is small and you know everyone personally. I used to find firing people very difficult and felt bad about putting someone, perhaps with a family, out of work. But you have to remember that there could be someone else out there who deserves that job and could do it better.

You also owe it to the rest of your staff to ensure they are working with the best possible colleagues. It is not fair on a team to force them to carry incompetent members. If you don't let go of people who are not up to the job the team will go downhill and so will the business. To create a top class business you must appoint, and keep, people on ability. The moment you don't, it is the beginning of the end for your organisation.

Decision making

"I'll get back to you on that". The boss who is always saying that and never does get back to people is a poor leader. Staff and managers quickly become frustrated with going to the chief for a decision and getting nothing but prevarication and delays.

Being a good leader means being decisive. It doesn't mean you will make the right decision every single time, but you will make clear decisions and take ownership of them.

In too many organisations people tell me about bosses who sit on the fence, can't make up their mind and put off decisions. Perhaps this is particularly a weakness of people who are promoted to the top job after years as middle managers, when they never had to take a definitive decision.

But staff become frustrated and cynical when they can't get a decision out of their boss. Indecisive chiefs lose all credibility and become a laughing stock with their own people. Morale suffers.

You may think you prefer to take your time on decisions, but I believe, nine times out of 10, the time you take to make a decision has no bearing on the quality of that decision.

In business you have to be quick to react, to seize the moment. Speed is always a competitive advantage. That is why small businesses can often do better than big ones because they are quick to turn on their feet. A good leader should be able to think fast and, with a clear view of where the business is going, should be able to make a decision on the spot.

Sometimes you need more information, but again, good leaders keep themselves informed. You should have systems for feeding through to you all the data you need, as I will explain in Chapter 11. If you do have to tell people you'll get back to them with a decision, make sure you do so and as quickly as possible.

People who have joined our organisation from other companies are astonished at how fast we make decisions. They find it very motivating that their boss is busy, but never too busy to get back to them with a decision.

A decisive leader can inspire good decision-making throughout the business. An organisation where people are not afraid to make decisions is an organisation that can keep moving forward. It is not weighed down by a backlog of questions waiting for an answer: issues are dealt with as they arise.

I find the decision-making part of the mind is like a muscle - the more you use it, the stronger it gets. The more decisions you make, the easier it gets.

As leader, you will constantly be hearing, "what do we do about this, boss?". Most of my top managers are good decision-makers themselves and they sort their own problems, but there are always questions they have to bring to me, which I must deal with on top of my own work. I can arrive in the office on a Monday, perhaps after a few days away, and inevitably there will be queries needing a response. But when I start I can be a decision-making machine, dealing with one after the other. And I deal with them amazingly quickly - it's like a ping-pong match and I really enjoy it.

So don't get hung up on decisions - enjoy the challenge and have the nerve to risk making the occasional wrong decision. Mistakes can usually be put right and you will have learned something for next time.

Decisiveness is one of my strengths. Even if I can't make a decision straight away, I don't push the problem aside. I enter it on to my work sheet, to be dealt with and I make sure I follow it through. Perhaps 10% or so of issues require some specialist input, so I take the advice I need before I make a decision. But, again, I do that promptly.

It takes the same length of time to make a decision whether you do it straight away, or leave it for a month. So make it there and then. The decision you make in a month's time will probably be no better than the one you make now - and it could well be worse. In the meantime your people will have been frustrated and rapidly losing interest in the issue as they wait to hear back from you.

One of the great aids to decision-making is certainly experience. Having been in business for 25 years, I now find there are few situations I cannot deal with, as the chances are I will have encountered this problem before. If I haven't, I can talk things through with the team of people around me.

Between them, they can contribute a great many skills and ideas.

My advice to new managing directors of our companies is to get as much experience under their belt as possible. The trick is to learn from other people's experience: to pay attention to what they are doing and why. David Robinson, my Group Managing Director, spent a lot of time learning from me in his early days. When I was not around and he had to make the decisions himself, he would ask himself how I would deal with the problem, and 99 times out of 100 this worked.

Good decision-making requires you to have a clear sense of what you want and where you are going. It all comes down to priorities.

As leader, you will be judged on your priorities. In fact, much of your day will be a process of continual prioritising. You are leading the organisation and you must decide what is important, in the light of your strategy and your information about what is going on around you, inside and outside the business.

Once you have decided the priorities, everything tends to fall into place. Decisions become easier. When people around you realise what the priorities are, they will work better and perhaps bring fewer problems to your door, because they can make a decision themselves.

Clear priorities will help you make the most of your time. I go into every meeting with an agenda written out, and I stick to it. I push the meeting along ruthlessly. If there is not enough time to cover the agenda, again I prioritise and focus on the essentials.

Priorities, of course, are changing all the time. What was important yesterday will be replaced by something new today; an issue which was minor a couple of weeks ago will suddenly become urgent. So the leader is constantly juggling priorities, in the light of information coming in. Even speaking on the phone you have to be asking yourself, "are we covering the important points"? The question always at the back of your mind should be, "am I doing these jobs in the right order? Am I dealing with the most important things first? What must I do next"? After a while, this becomes a reflex and you will be working at the peak of your efficiency.

You can't juggle all the tasks of leadership in your head and the invaluable tool here is my worksheet. I explain in Chapter 5 how I use this. The worksheet is not only a checklist for the things I have to do, but a way of ordering my priorities. Items move up the list and are carried forward from one week to the next. Jobs which were not a priority two weeks ago become a priority this week. Deadlines approach, something has to be done by tonight, you have a meeting tomorrow and must prepare for it and so on, in a continual process.

You must always be analysing in your mind what has to be done next. That is why it is so important to have your tasks on the one worksheet, so you can see at a glance all the things to pick from, like a menu. Throughout the day you must be deciding what is most important.

Delegating

To run a successful organisation you have to delegate.

This may sound obvious, but it is amazing how many able and ambitious people are reluctant to delegate. The sad fact is that, no matter how able and ambitious they are, if they do not learn to delegate they will never head a thriving organisation. They will stay a one-man band.

The chiefs who have most difficulty delegating are usually people like me - entrepreneurs who have set up their business from scratch. I started with one shop. The difference between me and all those who started with one shop and still have one shop, is that I learned how to delegate.

To do more - to develop your job and expand your business - you have to delegate.

I am a very busy person but I have a kind of laziness at heart: I have never wanted to do everything myself and most of the time I am quite happy to hand work over to someone else. As a child I thought I wouldn't achieve much, because I was lazy. But as soon as I found out that getting other people to do things for me meant I could do more, I could see the potential.

However, sitting back and letting everyone else do the work, regardless of the outcome, is a recipe for chaos. Delegating does not mean relinquishing control. This is a key lesson many leaders have to learn if they are to get over their inability to delegate.

Staff may think their boss does nothing but take long lunches while they do all the work, but the reality is that most leaders do too much work, rather than too little. Sometimes this is to do with poor time management, but usually it is to do with a failure to delegate.

Few of us have been trained to delegate. In fact it runs counter to the way we are taught as children. Most of us are encouraged to do things for ourselves and become self-reliant. All through our education we are tested on things we do ourselves and to get help from anyone else is seen as cheating.

So managing other people is not a skill we possess when we enter the world of employment. We assume that to be a good employee means doing our own tasks well - not running five people and achieving five times as much. We concentrate on the work we've been assigned, which has our name on it. When people are promoted to managers, they become uneasy. If they are not doing the work themselves, how can they be sure it is done properly?

I had to sort these things out for myself when I started my own business.

So many enterprises stay small because they cannot handle the transition of changing from an entrepreneurial business to a professionally managed one.

Growing from one shop to two is perhaps the most traumatic change a retail business can go through. It would be the same for a professional or a craftsman: to go from handling all the clients' work or creating all the products personally, to entrusting this to other people, is a huge step. Some very able people can never bring themselves to take that step.

You can run one shop yourself, whether you have two staff or 202. But once you have another shop or office you have to appoint a manager. You cannot be in two places at once so how do you maintain control? You have to set up systems. Delegating is not just about getting other people to do things: it is about getting the right people to do the right things, monitoring what they do and developing them so they can do more.

Having a good team of people to whom you delegate is essential. The leader of any sizeable company will have a finance director, marketing director and so on who are responsible for key tasks. Astonishingly, political leaders do not have this support. I was very surprised when I looked at the management structure of a minister's office and discovered ministers have only one person to whom work could be delegated, their private secretary. That means the private secretary is a minister's sole eyes and ears to the outside world - all work has to go through that one person. Furthermore, as a civil servant, the private secretary's boss is technically not the minister, but another more senior civil servant.

Ministers are expected to achieve so much, yet all the work they want done and all the information they want back is channelled through one person. If that civil servant is dynamic and good at their job, there may be no problem, but what if they are not? The minister is at risk of being inef-fective and ill-informed. I would question whether this is the best system.

Delegating is hard work. I find the difficult part is not so much giving out tasks, as following them up.

Delegating to people means managing those people. This is where I stick with my 'layers of 10' principle. No-one - even the head of an organisation - should be directly managing more than 10 or so people. It might be a dozen but it cannot be 20.

This is because effective management is hard work. To delegate successfully you need, not simply to hand work over, but to follow up with meetings, receive reports, give feedback, sort out problems if they run into trouble, chase up results and generally push, coach and develop your people.

It's hard work, but don't let that stop you delegating. Don't think "it would be quicker and easier to do it myself". If you hog all the work, your managers and staff will never develop and you will not be able to take the organisation - and yourself - forward.

One of the most important ways to progress as a leader is to let go. A good example from my own experience is that I always used to do the buying for Richer Sounds. I considered this was the key task for the success of the business and I prided myself on securing the best deals. Then came the day when I sent one of my managers to a buying meeting without me, and he came out with an improvement on my deal.

Once I had got over the blow to my ego, I realised how liberating this was for me. If I could hand over the buying, my pet job, I would be freed up to do so much more. The result has been that I have gone on, not only to expand Richer Sounds, but also to start other companies and build up a group. I could not have done that if I were still involved with the nitty-gritty of running Richer Sounds. I've been able to seek out new challenges. This is as important for leaders as it is for anyone else in the company. Just because you are at the top of the tree, it doesn't mean you have no further to go. You have to learn and innovate if you are to stay fresh and not lose your enthusiasm for the job.

The key to good leadership is achieving the right balance between maintaining control and letting go.

Narrow perfectionists tend to make bad leaders. There are some in every company: the ones who will go over and over a piece of work until it is right in every detail, but would barely notice the office burning down around their ears in the meantime.

People like this often have valuable skills, but the ability to run a business is not usually one of them. People don't like working for them, because perfectionists can't bear to delegate. Other people's work is never good enough and they'll take work back to finish off themselves. For staff this is soul destroying. Where an organisation has a high staff turnover, it is worth looking at the boss to see if they are this kind of character.

Successful chiefs are much more likely to be a jack of all trades. Being an effective leader is not so much about being a revered expert – it is much more like being one of those entertainers you see on the Generation Game, keeping 20 plates spinning on sticks and rushing round giving each stick a nudge when the plate starts to topple.

The leader does not need to be an expert in any one thing. There are always specialists there to handle the details. But the leader must know enough about all the aspects of the operations or the service in order to keep the whole show going.

If you find it difficult to let go – force yourself. Hand an important task over to one of your managers. Take a Friday off and see if the company falls apart when you're not there. It won't, and when you ask your staff whether it was OK on the day you didn't come in, they'll say it was fine. Then start taking Thursdays off, then perhaps one week in three. With your free time, expand the business, or start another business or spend more time with your spouse or take up mountaineering. However busy you think you are, you can fit more in if you train yourself to delegate properly.

It's very simple: you will never run a successful organisation and you will never get rich by doing everything yourself.

You may have highly sought-after skills and be able to earn a lot in a consultancy role. But you will still reach the limits, unless (as I have done) you employ other consultants and send them out to clients.

Delegating gives you incredible leverage. You only need four layers of 10 to run an organisation of 10,000 people - that was how the Romans ran their empire after all. Delegating means getting the right people to do the right things - and then leaving them to get on with it, while you move forward in other areas. You then follow everything up with your people and develop them so that they blossom and excel and your organisation blossoms too.

Chapter 4

Life at the top

My first day as head of my own business was one of the best days of my life. I remember sitting behind my desk, aged 19, thinking – "I'm in charge of my own destiny and it's wonderful".

I still think it's wonderful. But leadership makes unique demands on your life. It brings personal challenges, stress and enormous pressure on your time. You have to be prepared for these and find ways to handle them if you are to carry the role of leadership successfully.

Handling the task

The leader has a unique role. If you head your own company or have been a chief executive for many years, you may have come to take this for granted. But to understand what leadership requires, it is worth reminding yourself why the top job is different from any other in the organisation.

Someone who is promoted into the chief executive role, no matter how senior they were before, will immediately encounter this difference. It can be a real shock to the system.

To be a successful leader, you have to handle the demands of the job intelligently. You have great freedom, but also great responsibility. The success of the whole organisation ultimately rests on you.

So it is a very difficult job and often a lonely job; it is also a very exciting job, stimulating, rewarding and satisfying.

It is totally different from working for anyone else. Other managers, even senior directors, work to a structure. But the leader has no imposed structure - he or she has to create that structure themselves. The leader works from a blank sheet of paper.

Not all chiefs recognise this. If you look at how your organisation operates and find it is not following your strategy but does things the way they have always been done, or the way they "have" to be done - then you are not leading. You are merely occupying the top post. It must be your decisions that drive the business, and you take responsibility for the results.

I have seen very able managers within our group promoted up from running a shop to eventually running one of our companies. They are accustomed to taking responsibility, but they are staggered by how different it is to be running the whole show. Not all of them can handle it.

Managers normally have a defined area of work - a shop, or a region, or a finance department. When you are running the whole company you are faced with juggling all the different areas: staff problems one minute advertising strategy the next. You have to be able to switch from one to another, all the time keeping sight of the big picture.

Many of our people who started in the shops were surprised by the diversity of the managing director's working week. Instead of having the framework of the shop - opening at a certain hour, dealing with customers, the tasks at the end of the day - they were suddenly in an environment where each day was different from the next. They had to create their own framework and their own motivation, getting themselves charged up each morning.

Motivation of staff is hugely important in any organisation, as I have written about in my book "The Richer Way". As the leader, your job will be to motivate the 10 senior people working for you. But who motivates the leader?

This is a serious question. With luck, your own vision and your enjoyment of the job will be powerful motivators. But as I have often said, motivation has to be continually maintained, renewed and fed with fresh ideas. Think about how you apply that to yourself.

Reward is one of the motivators and you should be satisfactorily rewarded, or able to reward yourself. But financial rewards alone are not sufficient. People also need recognition, to be motivated. I often emphasise to managers the importance of a simple "thank you" to staff.

However, the chief gets very little recognition. You must work hard at giving it out to your people, but be prepared to receive little yourself. Few people think (or dare) to say "well done" to their boss. That is not a reason to feel hard done by – but it is a reminder of the factors that can lead to stress.

It can be lonely at the top, because you have no peers around you. Inevitably you must carry many problems yourself instead of unloading them on to someone else. Whom do you talk to?

In terms of work issues, I am lucky enough to have a group of people who have been around me for many years. As I am generally an open person, there is little I cannot talk about with my board members and closest lieutenants. I have developed a good team with whom I can throw around ideas and concerns.

It also helps to have wise friends in different businesses, outside your own company, with whom you can discuss important issues. This is particularly necessary if you are running a small business. There is great benefit in being able to talk with business or professional friends who know you well and whose views you respect. If they are not involved with your business, they can give you valuable objective advice.

Of course it is also hugely important to have support at home and among close friends. This is one reason why leaders must give themselves time away from the office. One of the best ways to be successful in your work is to have a full life outside work.

What kind of leader are you?

There are two main routes to the top: either you are heading a business you have built up yourself, or you have been appointed to the top job in an organisation.

Both entrepreneurs and professional managers can make equally good leaders. It is not your route to the top that makes you a leader but what you do when get there. But entrepreneurs and professional managers do tend to have different strengths and weaknesses. If you are aware of these, you can counterbalance your weaknesses. Once you recognise which skills you lack you can make sure you have people around you on the board who possess those skills.

In my group of companies we have a mixture of both kinds of managing director. There are people who came to me because they wanted to start their own business, and there are those whom we identified as exceptional managers and put in to head a new venture.

Entrepreneurs tend to have plenty of natural drive and a strong vision of what they want their business to be. These are essential qualities in a leader, but leadership requires much more than that.

Entrepreneurs often lack the discipline they need to make their organisation truly successful. They can be impulsive, impatient and moody (I include myself here!) and prone to taking their eye off the ball, with dangerous consequences for the company. Many, like myself, are not academic, which is fine – but that also often means they don't like figures, which is a big weakness when running a company.

Entrepreneurs often have an ambivalent attitude to leadership. One minute we are suffering from delusions of grandeur, thinking we are masters of our little universe, the next minute we are thinking of selling up and moving to a chateau in France.

Many of us feel a conflict between being entrepreneurial and being a manager. Being a manager has connotations of being steady and disciplined and perhaps boring, whereas we like to think of ourselves as risk takers, pulling off incredible deals, flying by the seat of the pants, going to China with a rucksack and coming back a millionaire.

The upside is that entrepreneurs can be very inspirational: they often win loyalty from their staff through their energy and the force of their vision. The downside is that they can be so carried away by the next idea that they do not listen to the needs of their organisation or the workforce.

Typically, entrepreneurs build their business up to a certain level and then sell it, get bought out or go bust and start all over again. The UK business world over the past 15 years is full of examples. But this pattern is not inevitable. Some entrepreneurs go on to run big companies.

It is certainly true that entrepreneurs and the City often do not mix. Entrepreneurs do not like the discipline imposed by the City. Most of us have never liked discipline – which is why we went off down the market to make money instead of sitting exams at school. We find it very difficult to present our business to a bunch of graduate analysts in suits who say our company figures aren't good enough.

When I am asked why I don't float my company, I say I don't want to be put on a fixed salary and told to cut my hair. Certainly if you do choose to go public with your company, you have to take the consequences and accept the rigidity. Richard Branson floated his company, didn't like it and bought it back. I have respect for him for that because he stuck with what was right for him.

The trick for entrepreneurs is to train themselves to be more professional and to assemble a board whose members supply the skills they lack. The Richer Group board is small but highly successful because we complement each other.

Professional chief executives can also make excellent leaders. They might never have wanted to start up a business themselves, but they can be just as innovative and inspirational.

In my experience, where professional managers can fail as leaders is that they cannot get to grips with the unique character of the job. I have seen people of great promise be promoted to the top job and then grind to a halt. With no-one telling them what to do, they don't know where to start. They don't know how to set the strategy and drive the business forward every minute of the day.

In my group of companies we are learning from mistakes. In the past we have appointed people to head up new companies without appreciating the size of the leap they needed to take from being a senior manager to managing director. Some could not handle the pressure and started making elementary mistakes that were completely out of keeping with their former competence.

The other question is whether a professional manager has the necessary drive. When they get the job of course they are full of enthusiasm and pride. But, as an entrepreneur, I am concerned whether someone running a company which is not their baby can ever have enough determination to get the business through bad times.

If they are good enough, I think both entrepreneurs and professionals can learn and develop the qualities needed to be a good leader.

Power with responsibility

The leader has tremendous power within the organisation and this must be used wisely.

It can be startling to realise how much influence you have over people. When I grew a pony tail half my staff sprouted pony tails! When I stopped smoking, many of my directors also gave up. So you have a responsibility to your people over and above the day to day responsibility and you must be aware of that.

The leader must be the social conscience of the organisation. This is not a job you can delegate. Absolute power corrupts absolutely and as the boss you are the person most at risk of abusing power. You are answerable to very few people, particularly in a private company. Even in a public company there would be few mechanisms to check you if you ever started to misuse your position.

By abusing power I don't mean only in terms of putting your own interests before those of the organisation. I mean overstepping the mark in the power you have over other people. Bullying is the sign of a bad leader. A certain degree of fear within an organisation is healthy. The centre of the organisation must be in full control and this discipline is maintained, to some extent, by fear: people must know they will not be allowed to get away with breaking the rules. But abusing that fear is very wrong.

Questions of image

For years, the only person I got my hair cut for was the bank manager. I've now decided I'm a valuable enough customer to get away with long hair, but I still change into a suit when we're meeting the bank.

Professional managers know this but entrepreneurs like myself have to be reminded that bank managers like to see them looking smart, as it shows some kind of personal discipline. People who have started up their own business often have the attitude that "this is me - take me as I am". That is fine, but when your business is still small, don't be too surprised if the bank turns you down for an overdraft when you turn up in jeans.

It is what you do as a leader that counts, not how you look, but it is worth thinking about your image: it goes hand in hand with how you think about yourself as the boss.

Appearance affects the way banks, customers and suppliers relate to you. They will lose respect for you if they see you looking scruffy because it implies you have no respect for them.

But it also affects your relationship with employees. This is particularly important in a small company where the atmosphere is informal. If you are fretting about getting your Armani suit dirty when you visit the factory, don't be surprised if your workforce thinks you are out of touch with them.

But if your staff only ever see you in jeans, they will assume you are aiming to be one of them and will talk to you accordingly. It is no good lashing out at them for being cheeky if you have been sending out the wrong signals.

Entrepreneurs tend not to be short back and sides people. We like to be rebels and appearance is one of the ways we do this. Maybe it is vanity - maybe it is one of the ways we maintain our drive and energy. Very often, people like having a colourful boss.

People sometimes ask me if I have deliberately cultivated the casual, long hair image. The truth is I like having my hair long and since I'm the boss, I can get away with it. Anyway, at my age if I got it cut it probably wouldn't grow again, so this is my last chance to preserve my youth!

I am aware that there are two sides to my image as leader. Our Richer Sounds staff are young, on the whole, and perhaps the way I look breaks down the distance they perceive between themselves and me as the Chairman. It is good for them to feel they are in a young-minded company. On the other hand, I want them to have respect for me. It is rarely a problem. Everybody knows I am the founder of the business, and there is a line of respect that people seldom cross.

Manners

Courtesy is very important. You cannot leave it behind just because you are the leader. We all make an impression on the outside world through the way we behave and the leader should be making a good impression, and setting a good example.

Good manners are the sign of a thoughtful person. Although my secretary arranges meetings, if I have to cancel a meeting, I ring up personally and rearrange there and then if possible. I hand write birthday cards and "thank you" letters and phone people myself if they're ill. It may not be strictly necessary but I think it's important.

I am very keen on my managers and staff showing courtesy. Our young sales assistants sometimes do not like wearing a shirt and tie in the shop, but we tell them it shows respect to customers.

The leader should treat everyone with respect, from the receptionist upwards - and not just in his or her own company but elsewhere. It means being polite to a supplier's secretary or to waiters when entertaining a client.

You can learn a lot about people from how they behave towards those with a more lowly status. When we are interviewing for a senior job, we do the cup of tea test – do they thank the person who brings them a cup of tea? It matters, because you should pay attention to the people who are doing you a service. This is particularly important if they have put themselves out for you.

Managing your time

As leader, you come under constant pressure. Managing your time is essential if you are to keep your sanity and run the organisation effectively.

Typically, the leader will be faced each morning with far more tasks than can be squeezed into 24 hours. The answer is often – go home.

Don't tie yourself to the office or the boardroom. Everyone has their own style of working. I would much rather work under intense pressure for a few days and then have time off. In my company we take a hard line against long hours. I hate a macho culture where everyone works until 9.00 in the evening because they don't want to be the first to leave the office. This does nothing for productivity.

In our shops and offices staff work a maximum five day week and there has to be a good reason for any exceptions to this. We expect people to work hard while they are in the office, but if they have completed their work by 4pm on a sunny day, nobody objects if they go home early. Our shop managers too, at quiet times of the year, can organise a four day week for themselves as long as the performance of the shop does not suffer.

In 1997 at Richer Sounds we changed the opening hours of our stores from 10.00 am till 6.00 pm to 12.00 noon till 7.00 pm. We did not force this on branches: each branch only adopted it if they voted unanimously in favour. Over the months, they all came round to the idea because there were clear advantages for both staff and customers.

For staff, their working day has been reduced by an hour, but we kept their take-home pay exactly the same. Opening at 12.00 means they can see more of their families, do some shopping or get a round of golf in and travelling to work is usually quicker and cheaper at those times. On the whole, they get home only half an hour later in the evening than they did previously. It is also more convenient for customers who, we found, prefer to shop in the evening when they have more time.

You have to commit yourself to maintaining a non-macho culture because, left to themselves, people will assume they have to work longer and longer hours. As chief executive, you must make it clear throughout the organisation what hours people are expected to work, and ensure that managers understand this.

You also have to apply this to yourself. If you are working crazy hours, senior managers will follow suit, in order to keep up or to prove their dedication. That will soon spread downwards until you have an exhausted and demoralised workforce. On the other hand, if you are working a nice six hour day, just check on what sort of hours the rest of your people work. If the organisation is surviving on massive amounts of overtime while you are having a round of golf, either you or the company is heading for disaster.

You will choose whether you work at weekends or keep them free. I like to have two days a week off and have at least one day completely to myself, when I am not on the phone and can take it very easy. On the other day I try to be more active, get some fresh air and do some work, such as reading reports, in peace and quiet.

You are the boss - no-one can tell you when to work, so make the most of that. Instead of giving up weekends to work at home, stay home to work some time during the week instead. Your spouse and family might appreciate it. You don't have to let work invade your home: protect yourself with a fax machine and an answer-phone at home so you can receive reports and messages without having to be available all the time.

Set an example. My staff see me work like a tornado, but know I also have time off. They know how full my diary is, so I don't feel the need to appear in the office just to show people I'm working.

Never hesitate to take time out during the day. Even a 10 minute walk each day can make a difference: take a break, have a change, vary your routine when you are in the office. Most of us would give this advice to our staff if we saw them working too hard and leaders should take this advice themselves.

It is important for you as leader not to get stale. You are the one that needs to come up with the ideas and the energy - that will be far more productive than working 80 hours a week.

Thinking and paper work are best done out of the office. On the whole, I keep the time spent in the office to a minimum. Administration and phone calls I can do from home. I limit myself to being in the office only when absolutely necessary - typically for seeing my managers or for meetings. Since I live in central London, I also hold meetings at home.

As well as managing where you work, manage when you work, to suit you best. If I have a tricky issue to tackle, like a complicated letter to write, or a particularly difficult problem, the best time of day to think about it is always the morning when the mind is like a still pond. By the end of the day it is like a turbulent sea and I would not be able to make a good decision. Rockefeller said never make an important decision after 6.00 in the evening and I agree.

Don't struggle with problems late into the evening. The more annoying the issue, the more reason to put it aside until the morning. I never deal with customer correspondence in the evening because it tends to get me uptight. If I do it in the morning, I will have forgotten about the problem by the end of that day. As the leader, you will have enough pressures on you, so develop ways to minimise the irritations. Why wind yourself up unnecessarily?

Have your hard, commercial meetings early in the morning. We start our buyers' meetings at 8.15 in the morning, when people are feeling grouchy and tough. In the afternoon people lighten up and relax, so we have our creative sessions, like marketing meetings, after lunch.

Organise yourself

Most leaders thrive on stress, to some degree - but there is a difference between stress which is stimulating and being so stressed out that you start to underperform.

The best way to cope with pressure is to be organised.

After I have spent a month visiting all the Richer Sounds branches before Christmas, I come back with masses of notes on all the ideas I have had and problems I have spotted. There is nothing more stressful than facing a pile of notes, messages and lists of things you are supposed to be doing. I find that by entering these on to my worksheet, ordering them and translating them from ideas and observations into actions to take, it calms the water. Once things are on my worksheet, I can see what I should be doing and can prioritise. I know I will be busy, but it takes the stress out of the situation.

My Mondays are a prime example of prioritising. I might have 11 inter-company meetings on a Monday, as well as letters to sign and phone calls to make. But I steam through the pile of things to do and don't rest until they are done. I am passionate about being up to date. I hate getting behind.

It is well known in the company that when I come in on a Monday, my desk is absolutely covered with paper for me to deal with, and by Monday night, my desk is absolutely clear. I have passed the work on to everybody else's desks. I am the arch-delegator and I'm proud of that. It means I have time for the real jobs of a leader – sorting out crises, putting out fires, but also talking to people, giving career counselling, looking at new business proposals. I am keeping all the plates spinning: some may wobble a bit but that's fine as long as most of them stay on the sticks.

The way I cope is through preparation. I can get through the work on a Monday because I have prepared my worksheet over the weekend. I write out my sheet, by hand, on a Saturday or Sunday so I can hit the ground running on Monday morning. I already know what my priorities are.

I am very thorough about preparation. The longer you spend on preparing for a meeting, the quicker you can get through the meeting and the easier it will be to bring it to a satisfactory conclusion. I never go into a meeting without a clear agenda and minutes from the last meeting, so I know exactly what I want.

Do your homework. If you are meeting suppliers, have the figures ready to hand about the performance of their product, so you are in a good negotiating position. In any meeting, having up to date figures at your fingertips puts you in a strong position, because the chances are the other parties will not have bothered, or if they have you can match them.

It is worth doing a bit of homework even for a social event. If I am going to a top notch dinner, I will get a list of the people sitting at my table, find out who they are and what they do. We may have a connection, or there may be someone it would be useful to meet with a view to doing some consultancy work for them. Most people realise the value of networking in business now, but for it to be effective, you need both to prepare and to follow up.

Minimise meetings

Most chiefs of an organisation will find huge chunks of their time are taken up with meetings. Do we really need so many?

Necessary meetings are internal meetings, meetings with people on the outside to consolidate or develop a business relationship or to explore the possibility of a new venture, and meetings with various VIPs who require your time and attention.

Then there are unnecessary meetings. Very many people will want to see you, because you are the boss, but do you need to see them? I find managing directors or sales directors of supplying companies are always knocking on my door. They want to deal with the boss and they're loath to deal with someone they see as an underling. I may meet them a couple of times a year, once to review business and perhaps at Christmas. But I deliberately avoid having regular meetings with them - not because I don't believe suppliers are important, but because I have delegated purchasing decisions. I am not the person who makes the decisions they want. If I met them, I would be undermining my purchasing director and buying group.

This is one of the benefits of delegating. You must be ruthless about letting go, or else people will not let go of you.

This can be difficult for people who have built up their own business, because their suppliers might have become long-standing friends. By all means meet them socially, but do not have unnecessary business meetings with them. I make it clear to our suppliers that I will not be meeting them, but I am still there for them. If ever there is a problem they can ring me, but I will not make a decision that undermines my managers. Never let anyone - customer or supplier - think they can override a decision further down the organisation simply by getting on the phone to you.

If a meeting is really necessary, try to make the other parties come to you. A massive amount of time is wasted by travelling to meetings. If someone really wants to see you, they can make the effort to come to you.

Even better, why not do business by phone or fax? I avoid as many meetings as possible. Too often you come out and realise you have spent an hour deciding something that could have been settled by two phone calls.

Always set a time limit on meeting. If someone is keen to have a meeting and you say, "I can fit you in but I've only got half an hour, is that OK?" they never say no. Almost nothing needs a two hour meeting. State at the beginning of a meeting that it will last an hour, and that way people don't waste 30 minutes asking each other about their holidays.

We have a tall table with no chairs in our office which we use for meetings. Business gets done twice as quickly when everyone has to stand up!

Lunches and dinners can also be a big drain on your time. Lunch takes out a huge chunk of the day and usually leaves you feeling listless for the rest of the afternoon. Dinners take an equally large chunk out of your home and social life. If you want to meet someone informally, why not breakfast between 8 and 9am or a drink after work between 6 and 7pm? Then you can keep the day free for the hard work. Instead of dinner, I often suggest an early supper, finishing at 8.30pm. That still leaves you with an evening at home.

The whole pattern of your working life is very important if you are to perform at the peak of your effectiveness as leader.

Be healthy

Leaders should not underestimate the importance of being fit and healthy to cope with pressure. If you are under a lot of stress, a brisk run beats Prozac every time. I say that as someone who hated sport at school. I had no interest in team games and on sports days I used to go round dealing in my hi-fis instead. I am still no fitness fanatic, but I find gentle, regular exercise is the best way to clear my head.

Running, swimming, cycling or just walking are the best things. The objection people raise is always lack of time. But as a leader, you ought to be sufficiently in control of your time to find 20 minutes twice a week to get some fresh air or go to the gym. It is not about building muscles: it is about feeling better and sharpening the mind.

Exercising and taking time out regularly is far better than resorting to artificial remedies to ease stress. Booze, drugs and crazy weekends with your mates all allow you to forget about work pressures in the short term, but in the long term they make you less able to cope with those pressures.

Chapter 5

Tools of the trade

To be an effective leader you must be organised. You should use all the techniques, tools, shortcuts and labour saving devices you can, to keep on top of your work.

By labour saving devices, I mean anything that saves time and enables you to do more. There is a whole kitbag of tools available to help you work fast and efficiently. The cost is usually very small in comparison to the value of a leader's time.

I once gave a talk to some very senior executives who had each paid £3,000 for a two day conference. I asked if they spent a lot of time in their cars and most said they did. I asked how many thought their time was worth more than £6 an hour and of course they all put their hands up. Then I asked how many employed a driver and only one man out of 200 put his hand up.

I questioned whether the rest of them had their priorities right. They were wasting time in the car when, for £6 an hour, they could have a driver and use their time for effective work, or, equally important, for rest. People are often reluctant to employ a driver, perhaps thinking it is pretentious. But he or she doesn't have to be in uniform with a peaked cap.

Using people's services to free you up for more important activities is highly cost effective. Some companies are prepared to hire executive jets to take their chiefs from one meeting to another. That's going a bit over the top but sometimes even that kind of expense can be justified. Do not under value yourself.

Employing a driver, or a diary secretary to save you spending hours fixing up meetings are good examples of what I call a labour saving device. I'm always on the lookout for anything that will save me time. Leaders should think about all the time-consuming little jobs that get in the way of the essential tasks, and find a way of getting someone else to do those jobs.

Over the years I have developed a toolkit to organise myself. Not only do these work well for me, but my managers use them too and so do many other senior people who have observed me using them. They are mostly low tech and very inexpensive.

The worksheet

This is the mainstay of my work. With this A3 piece of paper I am currently running 11 companies. I have developed the worksheet over the years and it is now foolproof. The main technical refinement, introduced a few years ago, was a clear plastic cover, to stop coffee being spilt over it.

The worksheet is one sheet of paper, with everything I need to do written out in lists. There is a huge amount of information on it, but I write very small, in a fine pen. The worksheet allows me to see at a glance everything to be done, and also to monitor whether things have been done or not. It enables me to delegate effectively, because it gives me dual information: first, the jobs I am giving to people, and second, whether the jobs have been done or not.

This one sheet of paper is more useful to me than a fancy computer. It can't crash, the information can't be deleted by mistake and its batteries won't run out in a crisis. Moreover, one sheet holds far more than a computer screen. The beauty of having everything on one sheet in front of you is that you can see what needs to be done and so you can prioritise – an essential leadership task.

I sit down every two weeks, usually at the weekend, and draw up a new worksheet on a plain piece of heavy-duty paper. This is a time consuming process, but by transferring information over from the old worksheet and writing up new lists, I am reviewing my work so that I am in touch with everything going on. As I go through the previous worksheet, I am checking up on what has been completed.

I rule the sheet out with all the columns I need. I'm continually adapting the layout, but the broad model stays the same. I typically carry two worksheets around, because in the short term there are always items outstanding from the previous sheet.

The worksheet starts in the top left hand corner with my two week diary. This is my short term diary: I also carry a long term diary. On the worksheet, the diary section has a line for each day and I draw lines through as the week goes on to show at a glance which day we have reached.

On each Monday's line I mark BN. That stands for "Be Nice", because Monday is such a hectic day and I am usually in a foul mood. I'm not sure BN works, but I try.

Mondays are always packed. As well as meetings in the morning and a pile of work on the desk, in the afternoon I see all my heads of department, which means 11 internal meetings. My people know not to phone me on a Monday morning and the same goes for most leaders. Anyone who is on the ball will be spending Monday in heavy meetings, going through last week's figures and seeing what's happening in the company. Someone who phones me on Monday with a call that could wait until Tuesday gets short shrift I'm afraid.

Every Monday I also mark "copy and signing". That means copying the worksheet, so that if I lose it I am not completely sunk. Signing letters is another regular task. All but a fraction of my letters are prepared for me and

I simply have to read and sign. It is invaluable to have an experienced secretary who can take a lot of administrative work off your shoulders.

Underneath the diary are columns for all the subsidiary companies, such as the consultancy business and the manufacturing company. There is a column for our charity foundation and one for the manager who liaises between me and all the subsidiary companies. There is also a list for new business opportunities which I am pursuing.

Below that are lists for domestic business and miscellaneous social activities. I keep lists for work to do at home in London, things to do when I'm in York at the weekend and things to do when I am out and about.

The long list is my ongoing jobs. As I tick them off I join the line up, so at a glance I can see what remains. Every item on the list is numbered and I mark an 'o' beside the things that have to be done in the office. Many tasks take a phone call, which can be made while I am out.

There are two columns for my diary secretary Teresa. Most items here are people with whom she needs to fix up a meeting or events to be arranged. She also makes my travel arrangements. Again there is a monitoring system: when I have asked her to do a job, that item gets a tick and when she has done it, I put a line through it. The length of the list shows how much work it is to arrange all these meetings, so how much time a good diary secretary can save you.

The column for Christine, my PA, has very different tasks. She does all my customer and personal correspondence, for example, and a huge variety of one-off jobs.

David Robinson, the Group Managing Director, also has a great many tasks and he is the only person for whom I have a back-up sheet. Because his jobs are often very long term, for example getting a property sold, they can't be ticked off every day and he might have 100 ongoing tasks. So as I give him a job to do from the current worksheet, I add it on to his separate sheet.

Other columns are all for key people: Claudia Vernon, the Group Marketing Director, Johnny Carr, Deputy MD, who deals with personnel and training issues, and Brian Proctor, the Purchasing Director.

I have lists for the meetings I chair, so that I can note matters to put on the agenda. There is our design group meeting; the "What Hi-Fi?" planning meeting, to draw up our advert; the buyers' meeting; and the catalogue planning meeting, which is also monthly.

The 'next' column is where I note items for the next worksheet. So if someone is on holiday for a week, I will put a follow-up note on that list. There is a pending list, for long term jobs; a list for my housekeeper in York; and matters to include both in the weekly reports and in my monthly video to the branches.

Other essentials
The other things I always carry around with me are a notepad and pen, plus my address book, diary and mobile phone which are all covered in yellow dayglo wrapping so that I don't mislay them in the back of a taxi. I did leave my diary down the back of an aeroplane seat once, and after that I came up with the dayglo idea. Also on the covers are the company phone number and the promise of a reward if found. Even my keys have a disc with a phone number so that if they are lost they will find their way back to me!

Pen and paper
The key to organisation is writing things down. I am never without my small memo pad and pen: it is in my pocket all day and beside my bed at night. I note down everything - ideas, questions, matters arising from a discussion or a phone call. I take it to dinners and down the pub.

I insist on my managers carrying their notepads everywhere. I have even tested them in a nightclub at one o'clock in the morning. Yes, they had their pad and pen with them. All our company directors who regularly work with me know better than to leave their pad and pen behind.

You cannot be organised and run a business if you don't carry a pad and pen around with you. I once spoke to a high-flying job applicant on the phone. He was recommended by a friend and his qualifications were good, but as far as I was concerned, he lost the job when he did not have a pen and paper handy to write down our company address so that he could send in his CV. If you are not organised enough to have a pen in your hand when you are making an important phone call, you are not up to the job.

Inside the pad I also keep business cards. I have two versions: one with my personal home and business numbers and one with business numbers only.

Diary

My long term diary is one month to a page so that, as with the worksheet, I can see everything at a glance. As I transfer items from the long term diary to the worksheet, I cross them off in the diary. Things that come up every year, such as birthdays, are marked in red. At the end of the year I go back and pick out all the red things and write them out again in the next year's diary. I enter my holidays in the diary at the beginning of the year. If you do not set aside time in advance, you will never get round to taking a holiday because so much work will get in the way.

I have the address book, diary and worksheet photocopied regularly: the worksheet at the beginning and end of the week, my diary once a week, and my address book every three months. Each week, my diary secretary gives all my managing directors a copy of my diary for the following week, so that they can see where I am if they need to contact me urgently. It doesn't hurt either for everyone to see my hectic schedule when I'm not in the office.

Emergency kits

It must be the boy scout in me, but I like to be prepared. I even carry a UK map on me, because I like to know where I am!

The Group Managing Director David Robinson and myself both have crisis plans for a range of situations. The plans cover a number of disaster scenarios, from death or injury to a customer, fire in the warehouse, through to adverse press reports or failure of the telephone system at our head office.

The plans contain step by step instructions as to what to do, the names and numbers of all the people to contact and so on. All the plans have been carefully thought through and are updated once a year. The idea is that it is a lot easier to draw up sensible plans when you are calm and rational than when disaster actually strikes. With the plans, we know we can respond effectively to emergencies.

I also keep a memo recorder in my tool kit. Dictating letters or reports can be a valuable use of time, for instance on a long journey or in a spare moment at home. The trick is to write the bullet points down, so that you are speaking to a structure, but without having to write the whole report first.

Using the phone

The phone is an indispensable business tool – as long as you do not become a slave to it. I have been appalled to sit in meetings with very senior people in other organisations and find that we are constantly interrupted by their phone.

You must have an assistant to field your calls, at least while you are in meetings. I give my secretaries the names of the few people for whom I will interrupt a meeting, either because they are VIPs or because they are hard to get hold of and I urgently need to speak to them. These names are put on a noticeboard in their office. Most calls are not that urgent and to take them during meetings interrupts the flow of thought and is discourteous to the other people in the meeting.

When you are making an important call, stand up. It is striking how much more businesslike and decisive you are when you are standing up. You will save yourself a lot of time with shorter, clearer phone calls. In my company, standing up for phone calls is part of the culture, so managers are not wasting their time on rambling telephone conversations.

Treat a phone call as you would a short meeting. If you prepare bullet points beforehand, you can be sure of covering all the important matters in one call.

Video

Few companies make much use of video internally, yet it is a simple and effective communications tool.

I like to put a personal message over to all colleagues in the company, yet I cannot go out and visit every branch each month. So instead, I send them a video.

This is produced in a low-tech fashion - basically, I stand in front of the camera and talk. I report on the branches' performance in the past month, comment on the highs and lows and announce any new developments. The face-to-face nature of a video means that this is a good way to motivate people: if a branch or an individual is praised, thanked or criticised on video, that has a big impact. People know it comes straight from the chairman and that their colleagues up and down the country will hear it.

I always follow up, so not only do we send out the videos each month, to be watched in each branch first thing on a Saturday, but we also check up on whether they have seen it. I include a code word somewhere in the video, which they have to enter on their weekly report to head office.

Managing director's pack

When we appoint a new managing director to one of our companies, we give them this ready-made toolkit in their welcome pack. The notepad and pen is the key item of course but there are also some more unexpected items, like the smoke mask, which could be a lifesaver in a fire in a hotel or on a plane. This also tells our MDs that they are valuable to us.

We also give them culture notes. Every business or organisation has its own culture and if someone is joining your company from the outside, they need to know the culture in order to be effective in the job. So our culture notes tell them what sort of company we are.

When we appoint a new MD, the group managing director spends a day going through the culture notes with them. The idea is to prevent unnecessary friction and mistakes because they are unfamiliar with the way we work. The advice comes under various headings: organisation - using the worksheet, time management, the importance of taking notes and so on; internal communications; financial information and control; working with me - what I expect from my MDs; dealing with the press; and so on, through to manners and presentation.

Chapter 6

Good times, bad times

Both success and failure are tests of a good leader. It is when a business gets into difficulties that leaders prove themselves – yet periods of success can be the more dangerous times for the leader.

Dealing with success

There are a number of things not to do when you have had a good year, seen the money flooding in, won an award or such like.

The first thing you don't do is to go bragging to the newspapers and have photos taken of you on a leopard skin sofa in your lovely mansion. Everyone, especially your staff, will think you are an idiot.

It is a natural temptation when you have done well and are proud of your success, to want to tell the world and have it recorded for posterity. By all means talk to the press – you probably have a worthwhile story to tell. But don't let it go to your head and make it seem as if the achievement was all yours.

It may be true that you have been personally responsible for the strategy that saved the business or turned round a failing organisation. But nothing could have been achieved without your staff, so make sure they get their due recognition. It is much better (and probably more truthful) to talk about a team achievement. That will boost morale within the organisation and enhance your image in the long run. Most leaders have a bit of an ego, but when times are good, you can afford to show some modesty.

The second thing to avoid is allowing the business to become overblown. In good times, there is always the temptation to grow too fast. People tend to think they can walk on water after they've had a few successes. In my first year in business, Richer Sounds broke even, in the second year we made a profit and in the third year I lost a small fortune because this success had completely gone to my head. I thought I was a hot shot businessman, whereas in fact I had got a few things right, more by luck than judgement. As soon as I started expanding the business and spending money like crazy, I fell flat on my face.

I never made that kind of mistake again, but several times in Richer Sounds' history we have had a good year and become complacent. We feel secure and start to spoil ourselves, letting the overheads mount. After a while we notice the business has become flabby and profits are down. We have to tighten up. In business as in life, pride does come before a fall.

So what are the right things to do? The lessons I learnt from those early mistakes are that when things start looking very good, sit down and analyse where this success comes from, instead of attributing it to your natural brilliance.

If you do not, the disaster can massively outweigh the success. In the early days of Richer Sounds, we made £20,000 profit in the first full financial year, but then managed to lose £130,000 in the next nine months.

The aim is to find out what you are doing right and do more of it. With Richer Sounds, I eventually found out where I was going wrong. We didn't have a competent bookkeeper, the books were a mess, and our external auditors were not right for us. So when we had a profit at the end of the year, we didn't know why. We later realised the apparent £20,000 profit was more of a snapshot of our financial position at that point in the year, rather than a true picture of our financial health.

It came down to lack of good controls. We did not have reliable, up to date financial reporting, so we had little idea of how the business was faring month by month. We were losing money through staff theft because of inadequate controls, but were not aware of it. If we had had good controls each month we would have detected the shrinkage earlier. Another major problem was that the business was not making enough profit: turnover was high but the margins were too low. But again, without good figures no-one was aware of this.

So, thinking the business was booming, I started expanding into more shops and more activity. I was not seeing management figures until the end of the year, so I could not understand what was happening when, nine months into the financial year, the business couldn't pay its bills. The reason was, it was losing so much money.

Our overheads were too high and I was not helping matters. I took a lot of money out of the business and bought myself a flash car and a bachelor pad. It was a classic mix of business immaturity and personal immaturity.

Twenty years on we're a lot wiser. We plan very carefully at the end of each year what we're going to spend the following year and we try to stick to that budget. When there has been a good year, it is easy to find lots of things to spend the money on, like opening new branches and refitting shops. But it is a mistake to be extravagant with capital expenditure. It can drain the cash, which is the life blood of the business, and run an otherwise profitable company into trouble.

We know Richer Sounds has its best years when it is not growing. When we are opening more shops, we tend to take our eye off the ball and profitability suffers. When we're consolidating and have a year when we do not open new stores or businesses, the profits tend to be better. So now we go up in steps: expand, then have a year of consolidation to earn the resources for the next phase of growth.

Success also has good and bad effects on the workforce. My company has a generous profit share scheme, so everyone automatically benefits from a good year. It is very important to enshrine this in a recognised scheme. Everyone knows what their share will be and they don't have to come cap in hand asking me. They also know that when we have a bad year, everyone will get less. Senior managers have a higher proportion of their salary paid via profit share, because they have to take more responsibility for performance. When the company does well, they do very well, which is a good incentive, but they also take the risk of seeing their salary drop if we have a poor year.

But even with profit share, people inevitably push for more after a good year. All of a sudden managers want bigger cars. It is the job of the person at the top to remain disciplined and not allow an explosion of spending.

Paradoxically, it becomes less easy to motivate people when times are good. I find people work better when things are tough: there's a siege mentality, they are ready to batten down the hatches and fight for survival. As long as staff believe in the company and don't think the chief is siphoning all the cash into a secret fund in the Caymans, they will usually give of their best in difficult periods.

On the other hand, in good times, you are likely to have a lower turnover of staff. People feel more secure if they know the company is secure, and the prospect of better pay and a good profit share works as a natural anchor.

Traditionally at Richer Sounds, we have been fairly mean with capital expenditure. I want to put money into people, rather than buildings. We have built up a reputation based on fairly small shops in fairly cheap locations – which reinforces the message to customers that they are getting good value. It is only in recent years that we acquired a large central office building, but even that is in an unfashionable corner of London.

Of course you have to spend more as a business gets bigger. But one of my principles is: 'under promise, over deliver'. In my companies we don't promise customers the moon, but we aim to surpass their expectations in terms of the service we give. One of the dangers of success is that, as your shops or offices get bigger and smarter, so customers' expectations will rise. Can you meet those expectations?

Trappings of success

They say bank managers start to worry when they visit a company's head office and see fountains in the lobby, a marble tiled private bathroom for the board and a photo of the chairman's yacht on his desk. That company is heading for impending doom!

So if you find yourself hiring a commissionaire for the door and looking in the Rolls Royce showrooms, just take a moment to wonder whether success is going to your head. Most of the money spent on a Rolls could be invested much more profitably elsewhere in the company. We have a wonderful fleet of cars (including a Rolls Royce) - but they are used by the staff. Each month the top performing Richer Sounds branches win the use of a luxury car. It is a motivation device that has never ceased to appeal, and has become almost one of our trademarks.

I have seen many leaders fall victim to the success syndrome. All of a sudden they see themselves in a new light - they're top people so they've got to have the right clothes and the right holidays and the right luggage to take to the right exotic destination. I am all for enjoying my money, but I don't kid myself I need to keep up with some high-class Joneses.

The worst danger for chiefs is that they take their eye off the ball once they feel successful. They start hobnobbing with the great and good. Being seen at Glyndebourne, Ascot and Henley becomes more important than leading the company. Going shooting becomes the main priority of the week.

Some leaders do have a problem about status. They pamper themselves to soothe their insecurities, and usually make themselves look foolish. Everyone has a laugh at the four foot tall millionaires who step out of enormous limousines.

I'm not saying don't have a smart car. But the trappings of leadership must be proportional to the success (or otherwise) of the business. I hear bosses say "people expect me to have a Ferrari". Who are they kidding? If you can afford it and you've always dreamed of having a Testarossa, fine. If you're zooming around while the company is struggling, don't think that the Ferrari will persuade your workforce that you are a brilliant and inspirational leader.

But equally, don't try to hide from your employees the fact that you have a nice lifestyle. They will always find out about the car and the yacht in the end. You could be keeping up an elaborate pretence of poverty while they snigger. My staff know perfectly well that I have a big house in the country, because they have all been there on training courses.

Having money is nothing to be ashamed of, if you have earned it through the success of your organisation. I believe business people play a useful role in society, providing employment and putting money into the economy. I pay taxes and what I do with the rest of my money is my choice.

Profit should not be a dirty word. Profit is necessary for a business to continue and develop. A strong leader will put the message over clearly to the workforce that the business is here to make a profit, but in an ethical way.

Being in business is often derided in Britain. A lot of business leaders are seen as soulless and greedy people, "fat cats". But it doesn't have to be like that. A caring business person, a benevolent employer, is not necessarily a contradiction in terms. There are business people with a genuine conscience, like Anita Roddick, a personal friend of mine, who cares passionately about everything she does and the effect on the environment and society. She has her critics in the City but I respect her integrity enormously.

I'd like to encourage more genuinely caring people to go into business, because it is a real way of making a contribution to society.

I try to put this message over to our own people. At our "virgin" seminars, I tell new recruits that when they go down the pub and meet mates who greet them with snide remarks about working in business, they should stand up and point out the important part they have to play in society.

After saving lives, creating quality jobs is surely one of the most crucial things you can do for people. Anyone who has been unemployed knows how ghastly it is. I do create, I hope, secure, stimulating, decently-paid jobs – and hundreds of them.

Secondly, business contributes through taxes. My mother wanted me to be a doctor but I faint at the sight of blood. However, the tax I pay must support at least 50 doctors. My companies, myself and my employees together pay huge sums in taxation and I'm proud to contribute to public services in that way.

Thirdly, my companies are efficient and offer good value for money. We don't cheat our customers and we enable them to save money, which could be put to good use elsewhere.

Finally, we also recycle 22% of our profits: 16% goes back to colleagues via profit share, 1% goes to the hardship fund to help them personally when they need it and currently 5% goes to our charity foundation, which puts money back to society through a variety of schemes. We don't do charity work to boost our image (we always give anonymously) – we do it because we believe in it and think we have something to offer.

When you are at the top, you can become a target for criticism. It is a British trait that people are envious of success. Learn to live with this and don't be defensive. Both reactions to success – extravagance on the one hand or embarrassment on the other – could lead you into making some silly decisions for yourself or the business. The most important thing is to communicate to your managers and staff, your customers and, if necessary, the business world at large, that your expenditure is in proportion to the performance of the organisation.

Handling your earnings

Managing directors and chief executives should have a low basic salary, supplemented by a large performance-related element.

All the managing directors of companies in my group have part of their salary as a percentage of their company's profits. One managing director is on 50% of profits. From my point of view, he is taking a very high proportion, but I agreed because without him, that company would not exist, and I would rather have 50% of something than nothing at all. The person who puts the money in and takes the risk should be able to take a profit.

Entrepreneurs should take as much money out of their company as the company can afford. It is a waste to have your money in the bank earning 3%. Banks always want you to keep your money with them so they can earn from it, but you can do much more with it elsewhere. You should be taking surplus money out of your business, to put into other companies. That way you do not have too many eggs in one basket.

Each year we estimate what profits the business is likely to make, then we downgrade that figure, to be cautious. We take away what the business will need for the year, in terms of capital investment in new branches, or a new computer system, and the percentage for profit sharing and the charity foundation. We allow for the money the bank wants left in and what remains is the amount I can take out.

If you are the private owner of a business, however small, think about what to do with your new found wealth. My aim is to build my personal wealth but also to expand my group of companies, roll out my philosophy to the wider world and be more involved in the charity sector. Wealth is also power and influence and you have the opportunity to use that.

Some companies do need to reinvest every penny of profit they make. If you are planning to double in size every two or three years, clearly there will be no surplus cash to take out. But with Richer Sounds, I deliberately grew the business slowly, because it is stronger that way.

This is an important decision to make. If you are intent on major growth, perhaps because other investors are driving you or you want to float the company, there is a cost to this. Make sure you realise it could be at the expense of a more fulfiling and varied life for yourself.

As a practical tip, I have also bought quite a lot of property, some of which I then let back to the business. This is a super-efficient use of wealth. Rather than the company buying property with its own cash, I give myself a bonus to buy the property, taking out a loan for the difference. I rent it to the company and the income pays back the loan, usually within five to ten years. I end up with a property in my own name, paid for, which continues to earn rent. I have both a nest egg and a large rent roll.

Setting up new companies

One of my aims is to invest in new business opportunities. This is always risky, but my experience is that the risks overall do pay off. I never put in more money than I can afford to lose.

Successful entrepreneurs take risks. But starting up new businesses is not as hazardous as it appears. If you invest a limited £50,000 each in 10 businesses and nine fail, you've lost £450,000. But the one business that succeeds can make millions. Usually the success rate is more like 50%.

Ideally, you should invest "limited amounts". If you invest by writing a cheque for £50,000 and handing it to someone starting up a new venture, your losses will be limited to that £50,000. The problem comes when you start a new business and you're paying its bills every week. It's easy to lose track and find thousands of pounds have gone up in smoke.

In recent years I invested in a small chain of keyboard shops. The business was disastrous and over three years I lost £450,000. But I also set up a manufacturing business. This lost money in the first two years but we stood by it. In year three it came right and in year four it is projecting a profit of just under £1 million, which means the company is worth £5 - 10 million. That pays for a lot of keyboard shops.

Knowing when to pull the plug is crucial, but not easy. It is important, right at the start, to set a limit on how much you will put into your new venture. When you reach that limit, you face the dilemma of whether to pull out and lose the lot or to put in more. This has to be a commercial decision. I always look at the trend. Even though the manufacturing business was losing money in the first years, the trend looked promising: the managing director was learning, improving his team and his product range, delivering on time and demonstrating other encouraging indicators. If these trends are not present, you have to be ruthless about pulling the plug.

There is always an issue of how involved you should be in the running of your new businesses. It depends on the situation: the needle swings from 'no interference' to 'major interference', according to how the new company is performing.

So when I invest in a venture, it will have a business plan and if it performs to that plan, I don't interfere - the needle hovers around zero interference. I am too busy to get involved in businesses which are doing perfectly well without me. But as problems start to occur and the figures don't come right, I tighten my scrutiny of the company. The head of the new venture will find me or my senior directors constantly on their back, demanding action. In the end they may find it unbearable and certainly I have had people give up their new company, complaining I was too interfering. But I only got involved because it was clear the business was in trouble and its managing director couldn't cope. When we set up new businesses we make it clear to the MD that this is what our regime is like: if they get it right, we won't interfere. But I won't stand passively by and watch my cash being poured down a black hole.

Entrepreneurs should not be worried about failure, as long as they learn from it. As long as the downside is quantifiable and the upside is unlimited, you can afford some failures.

There have been times when a business has failed, but it has not been a waste of time and money because I learnt a lot from the experience. What I learnt I can put to good use in all the other existing and future businesses. As long as you are learning and not just losing money blindly, it is not a disaster to have little businesses that don't work, if there are benefits to the rest of the group.

Not all successful ventures are worthwhile. I quantify my time and know how much my day is worth. All entrepreneurs should do that, so that they can take a view on the merits of new businesses. If the businesses you are running are making, say £10,000 a day, there is no point in spending two days a month on a venture that can only make £50,000 a year.

There are exceptions - if it is a venture you really enjoy or is worthwhile, like a charity, or if it has considerable future growth potential. There may be businesses from which you do not get a salary, but which grow in value by so much a year, which can be worked out as a daily rate.

Of course, I speak from experience and for small enterprises, wanting to start up their first subsidiary, the risks may seem scary. But you have to start somewhere. The most important thing is never to invest more than you can afford to lose. So if you're a small business and want to try new ventures, take the plunge, or else you will not go forward. In my company we try things every day. Failure is not a dirty word in my organisation.

The critics will focus on your failures but do not let that discourage you. You don't need 100% success in starting businesses and you won't get it either. But keep going and one success will make up for several disasters that you have to mark down to experience.

Dealing with hard times

Steering your organisation through difficulties is the test of a true leader. As the figurehead for staff, customers and suppliers, you must remain calm and strong, no matter how great the pressures on you.

At times like these, the leader has to deal with both hassle and despair. These are two very different causes of stress.

Hassle

When people are queuing up to see you, the phones are ringing, there are half a dozen customer complaint letters on your desk, you have to leave to catch a plane in 20 minutes and you feel as if your head is about to explode - that's hassle.

The individual problems might be minor, but when they come one after another and you haven't enough time to sort them all out, hassle can really push you to the edge. It can be a serious problem: if unchecked, eventually nothing goes right and you finish up punch drunk at the end of the day, dreading going into the office tomorrow.

All managers have hassle, to some extent, but for the leader it is vitally important not to succumb to the pressure. You may have had a deal fall through, or have just come from a series of bad phone calls, but when you walk into a meeting or into one of your branches, you have to put all the hassle behind you. You have to wipe the slate clean and you may have to do this several times a day. You must be there to listen to your suppliers' or your staff's needs, not unload your bad mood on to them.

It is important to develop the skill of putting on a brave face. Once again, it comes back to determination. Hassle can feel like being hit over and over again: you wonder when it will stop. Only grit and determination will see you through.

To prevent hassle, you need to get organised. Problems will always arise. But if you are efficient in planning, organising, delegating and letting go, you will give yourself the time to sort out the problems, instead of letting them get on top of you. Every leader should automatically build in time for fighting fires.

Don't add to your hassle by allowing interruptions. On the whole, I have an open door policy. My door is not literally open, because the office gets noisy, but I have a sign on it saying "Don't knock - please enter". I find knocking more irritating than people coming in unannounced. But everyone knows that on a Monday I will be incredibly busy and in a foul mood, so I don't want interruptions then.

A clear desk is important. I always worry when I see a chief with a messy desk: it indicates a disorganised mind. At the beginning of the day you are bound to have a ton of paper on the desk to deal with, but at the end of day, the work should either have been delegated and be sitting on someone else's desk, or it should be in neat piles, ordered and prioritised. It's a question of mind set. You cannot make the right decisions if there's no order. You need to know that everything is there, no items of work lost or forgotten, before you can prioritise.

Despair

Despair is different from hassle. It is what you feel when you look at your monthly cashflow figures and see you need £2 million more than your overdraft limit.

Despair is when you see the company going down hill and there seems to be no way to stop it. It is a kind of drowning feeling. It seems the waters are closing over you and you cannot save yourself.

Experience has taught me that it is possible to pull a business back from the brink of disaster, but it can only be done by leading from the front. You must have the determination that you are going to deal with this crisis and sort it out.

There is no way organisations can be successful if their leaders do not have that fire in their belly. They must have a passion for the business, a lust for success that enables them to lead the company out of failure.

My two periods of near disaster with Richer Sounds have shown me that it is possible to turn things round, however bad the situation. I had to be determined to the point of ruthlessness, with myself as well as the business. I had to make some hard decisions about cutting costs, which usually means reducing the size of the workforce. When Richer Sounds ran into trouble in the early days, the first thing I did was sell my flat and move into a smaller place. I stopped drawing a salary out of the company, as fortunately my wife was able to support me at the time.

Sometimes it will come to a tough decision about cutting the workforce. If you've got 100 people and cannot afford that wage bill, but believe you can pull the team together and get them to work 10% harder, you may have to lose 10 people for the sake of the company and the other 90 jobs.

To lose jobs, the first resort will be natural wastage. A failing company will often have high labour turnover. The next option is voluntary redundancy and if you're going to save money, you can afford to pay people off with a decent sum.

But in a smaller organisation you ought to know who deserves to keep their job and who hasn't been pulling their weight, so it might be better to make the decision yourself, rather than lose the more dynamic people, capable of getting another job, through natural wastage.

It is no good saying "I'm going to go bust if I don't deal with this" and then dodge the tough decisions. Companies are usually going down the drain because their expenses are too high. Quite simply, this means costs have to be slashed. A good leader will bear the brunt of that. A bad leader will take the easy option and declare bankruptcy rather than make any personal sacrifices.

Whether it is your own company or not, you cannot whinge about how bad times are unless you are prepared to do something about it yourself.

Bad times are subjective. With the benefit of experience, I can now handle difficult patches that would have other people tearing their hair out. It is vital to have good management information so you can see difficulties coming and judge how bad they really are.

Leading the workforce through bad times

Never try to hide difficulties from staff. They are often very aware when there are problems in the organisation. You must have an answer if someone asks whether there is a problem. I cannot remember ever not telling a colleague the truth about the state of the business.

It is rare that any harm is done by telling the truth to people. Many companies are scared of giving their staff any figures, in case the true situation "got out". But I tell them, most of their staff probably already know the true situation – including those ones who are leaving you to join your competitors. If people want to find out they usually think of a way.

We are open about figures in general, whilst making it clear to people that these are confidential. Very rarely have we been let down by colleagues disclosing information outside, but we get a huge positive boost to our credibility by being honest with people.

Other companies assure me they can't tell their staff that times are tough because people will just want to leave. But I find people aren't like that. If you say "We've got problems and we're going to sort them out", people will stick with you. As long as you are honest and take the front foot with bad news, so that they don't get all their information from gossip and innuendo and they don't fear redundancies in the middle of the night, staff can really display their loyalty during bad times.

The answer to despair is not to let the buggers get you down (I don't mean the staff!). I'm not saying that deals with every problem, but most problems have a solution somewhere. It doesn't have to be a brilliant solution – you just need the determination to carry it through.

If you can't pay your bills, work out which creditors will let you take a bit more time to pay, probably paying a little more interest. Next, phone up the credit controllers and negotiate. Then speak to some other banks, before you go to your main bank, so you have a plan B before they say "sorry we're pulling the plug". Then go to your bank and think what security you can offer them in the short term.

These things are all feasible, although you don't know that when you have not been in business very long. The first time you find you can't pay your bills, it is terrifying. You feel like jumping out of the window. But don't jump - think!

Most people who are successful in life are simply the people who haven't let go. They stayed on the bus when others got off.

It took James Dyson, the vacuum cleaner inventor, 15 years to get his idea into production. He had been turned down by everyone before he went ahead and did it himself. If he hadn't been prepared to put his home and everything he had on the line, he wouldn't be sitting on a £250m company today. He could have got off the bus at any stop and he stayed on 'til the end.

To cope with despair you must put it out of your mind while you tackle the problems. Don't even think about failing. Keep fit and sane, and don't give up.

Chapter 7

Driving the business forward

A business should be moving forward all the time. In the marketplace you have to keep ahead of the competition, trying out new ideas, improving profitability. Even if your organisation is one that doesn't have to worry about market share, it still has to move forward. The search for better products, better ways to serve the customer and more efficient procedures is a never ending one. Once you stop, the business will stall and quickly start to decline. Your staff and customers will become disillusioned.

So who keeps the business moving? The leader.

The things that the chief really believes in and wants to happen are likely to be the things that do happen. Your people will see your priorities and make sure those things get done. So you have to be clear about what the goals and priorities really are. These are not decisions that can be delegated, otherwise the organisation will meander along aimlessly, or else be pulled in different directions as managers all have their own ideas about where the business should be going.

There are two mechanisms for driving the business forward. One is the strategy: the macro scheme pushing the organisation towards certain goals. The other is the micro scheme of continuous improvement. This is kai zen – a Japanese term that means "good change". It involves the daily search for better ways of doing the job. Even though this is about the fine detail, it is still the leader's job to lead the process of continuous improvement.

Strategy

Most leaders would agree that devising the strategy for the organisation is their responsibility. In fact in my company, drawing up the strategy every year is very much a group effort with the board. We collect a lot of input from colleagues and advisers and bounce ideas off each other. But in the end, the leader must put his or her name to the strategy.

The first part of drawing up a strategy is for the senior people to agree what the mission of the business is. The mission statement is really the strategy written down in simple, general principles. The mission statement gives everyone in the organisation the same goals. It tells you where you are trying to get to and the task every year or every month is to draw up a map of how to get there.

At Richer Sounds, our mission statement never changes but the way we fulfil it changes. For example, we want to give our customers value for money. Of course we change our product line, particularly as hi-fi is a very technology-driven market, but we always choose our products and pricing with that aim of value for money in mind.

So the strategy has to draw on many different elements: product innovations, different retail formulas, customer demands, staff ideas, movements in the market, economic trends, ideas gleaned from networking contacts and so on.

Every January, the Group Managing Director and myself sit down and talk through all this information and what it means for the business. Then we set out our goals for the coming year. A strategy must be formulated. It is not much use if it exists only as some vague and shifting thoughts in the leader's head. A strategy is not a state secret: it has to be communicated.

We pick out the 10 issues to concentrate on for the year. One of those is always "keep the fun" while other key issues vary year by year. Fun always has to be a goal because it's hard work. I believe that for people to be motivated at work, there has to be fun. That is why we have holiday homes, days out and a variety of rewards, large and small, for our staff. But it is human nature that fun ideas lose their novelty after a while as people get used to them. So bosses have to keep thinking up new ways to have fun. I thoroughly enjoy this. Since "The Richer Way" came out we have added a few more holiday homes - in Amsterdam, St Tropez, Marbella and Paris. This is what I mean by continually moving forward.

The strategy is cascaded down through the company on our layers of 10 principle. All the departments and branches have their own 10 goals for the year. We also draw up a business plan, which incorporates detailed ambitions for each department and each branch.

At the end of the year we go back and see how far we achieved our 10 goals. We don't always reach every goal, but this does not mean the process is not worthwhile. The fact of having an aim has already had an effect on the business.

Strategies and business plans must not be set in stone. We change our strategy many times. During the year we will adjust, tweak and revamp it. I talk to colleagues to get feedback on how the strategy is working out and whether we are getting to where we want to go. Sometimes we agree, sometimes not, sometimes I change the strategy as a result and sometimes I don't. But the whole thing is moving, the business is bowling along the road.

Innovation will mean different things for different organisations, but businesses cannot stand still. In hi-fi retailing that is obvious, because technology develops and new products come on to the market. Other kinds of business might have to generate more of their innovations themselves. Some companies lose their way because they don't change with the times and all of a sudden they find their products or services have been superseded. They have been left behind.

The leader should be thinking about this and researching what is happening, not just with direct competitors but more widely in the business world. You must be continually looking at the way you do things, continually being critical and restless and always prepared to make changes to improve.

Energy

The other way that you, as the leader, drive the business forward is through your energy and determination. Energy is vitally important for a leader. Your energy will inspire the people around you and flow through the company: it can make all the difference between an organisation that is drifting or stagnating and one that is going somewhere. I am naturally an energetic, restless person, but energy does not have to be manic activity A calm and considered energy can be just as effective in constantly pushing the business forward.

This energy will come from your belief in the business, your enthusiasm for your work and your determination to make it succeed. If you can convince your managers and staff of this determination, it will boost their motivation. People believe in a leader who believes in the business. They look to a leader for energy and inspiration above all, and want to see a leader who is going to make things happen.

The leader drives the business forward by pushing people that little bit further. I chair a number of key meetings in my company, such as the buyers' meeting and the meetings where we deal with our two main promotional tools – our catalogue and our hi-fi magazine advertising. After 20 years I don't need to do this. We have a good buying team and a good marketing department. Perhaps it sounds as if I am not letting go and allowing people to get on with their job. But I am not interfering with their job: I am pushing them to do their job better. That is my job. My involvement is a message that buying and marketing are crucially important areas and that we must never get complacent in these areas. We must keep doing better.

I chair these meetings because I enjoy it and because I have something to bring to them. I can push things along by asking questions. Is that the best advert we can do? Was that the best deal we could get? Can we do better? Is it head and shoulders above the competition? If not, why not? It becomes a personal challenge but I love this challenge. I really want my business to be the best and to stay the best. You can't stay at the top without working at it continually. Creating a successful business is not like constructing a building, which once it's up, stays up. You have to keep going forwards or you slip back.

I drive people all the time because I don't accept excuses. When a branch tells me they had a bad week because the weather was bad I tell them to look down Oxford Street or their nearest high street. There are always people out there spending money, whatever the weather. Our job is to make sure they spend money in our shop.

It's very easy to find excuses for under-performance. The weather's too cold - people are staying indoors, it's too hot - they're all at the beach, there's a big football match on, consumer spending is down and so on. I'm not interested in excuses. I want to know: are we attracting people into the branches? When they come in are we serving them as best we can and is every customer leaving the shop happy? I not only ask these questions but monitor and analyse the answers.

Driving the business forward also means keeping up the motivation - the praise, thanks and recognition that are easily neglected. The leader must be the one who does not take people for granted.

I am always searching for new ways to recognise and reward staff, particularly those people who do a lot of steady hard work without many opportunities for glory. I make time for them. For instance there's the Five Year Club, for members of staff who have been with us for more than five years. Every year I take those colleagues who have completed their five years of service out together for a big lunch at the Savoy or the Ritz. We also take all long-serving colleagues on holiday every year, maybe three days youth hostelling. At senior management briefings I'm the one who stands up at the end and not only congratulates the directors for working so hard but also reminds them not to forget the branches. Motivating people is hard work - once again the energy has to come from the leader.

Kai zen

When we draw up our strategy every year, one of our 10 goals is always to continually improve the business. This is one of the leader's most important responsibilities.

Kai zen - continuous improvement - is essential if you want your organisation to go forwards, not backwards. But what does it mean? Continuous improvement is not the same as, for example, increasing sales. You can boost sales by discounting all your stock, but it won't improve your business. Kai zen means doing everything your business does a little better, every day. It means constantly examining your strategy and processes to improve margins, to develop more attractive products offering better value for money and to find ways of allowing staff to work more efficiently.

This is about detail but, as I've said, the leader should never be too big for details. It will be the constant drip feed of small adjustments and improvements that keeps your organisation ahead of the pack. To make your business the best you've got to keep your edge sharp. Kai zen is a daily sharpening process.

To be open to continuous improvement, an organisation must be flexible and adaptable. It must be the opposite of the workplace where procedures are set in stone and people are forever filling in meaningless forms and carrying out purposeless processes because that's the way things have always been done. In my company we have a strong strategy and firm goals but nothing is set in stone: there is always an access point so the strategy can be tweaked and improved throughout the year. Kai zen is about evolution not revolution. It means ensuring your organisation can grow and respond to changing situations.

The reason this must be the leader's responsibility is that kai zen needs a strong drive behind it. Left to themselves, people tend to settle into safe and comfortable procedures and stick with what suits them, rather than discover what suits the customer. The leader must be there, keeping staff and managers on their toes and shaking them out of complacency. This is your role, to challenge, prod and question.

It is also your role to ensure that, when improvements emerge, they are implemented consistently throughout the company. The person at the top must do this, to avoid having, say, one branch or department coming up with a good idea but not sharing it with anyone else. If there is a better way of doing things, everyone should be doing it that way. You might have a thousand new initiatives across the company, but unless these can be applied throughout the organisation, there is no continuous improvement. Control from the top is essential to ensure that improvements are not just isolated and local.

In my company we go to a lot of trouble to develop very clear procedures, because we believe there is one best way of doing everything – until a better way is found. The leader must see that the search for a better way goes on.

You don't have to come up with all the ideas for improvements yourself. You probably will do so at first. If you have been newly appointed as chief, you will have many ideas for change. Equally, when you have your own business, while it is fairly small you are constantly spotting things that could be done better. But as your company grows, you cannot be in touch every day with every part of it. Furthermore, you will have managers and staff, each of whom could have original and useful ideas. This is a resource you need to tap into.

The way to do this is with a suggestion scheme.

The oil well

A good suggestion scheme is like having an oil well in your back garden. It is a source of ideas for improving the business and, if it is run properly, it won't dry up. Richer Sounds' suggestion scheme has been going for 10 years and the flow of ideas has never stopped. Before I introduced the suggestion scheme, I came up with most of the ideas for improving the business myself and that put a lot of pressure on me. Now 90% of the ideas for continuous improvement come from staff.

A lot of organisations get suggestion schemes wrong. So you, as the leader, must ensure you have a scheme that works.

The mistake many companies make with suggestion schemes is to give reward only as a percentage of money saved or generated by the suggestion. This leads staff to believe that the only ideas wanted are those for big, revolutionary schemes. This is wrong. Continuous improvement is not necessarily anything to do with saving money. Sometimes a better way to do things is more time consuming or costs money to implement, but will be worth it in terms of a better service to customers or greater efficiency in the long run.

The ideas I want from staff are about the small but important things that will help them do their job better. I want to hear about the things I won't spot for myself, because I am not there in the shop or the warehouse every day.

To attract the ideas you want, you must reward them. So you need to reward little and often. We assess ideas quickly and reward straight away. We give a minimum of £5 for every suggestion we receive, provided it isn't abusive or something staff should be doing anyway. Motivational rewards up to £25 are tax free so the employee clearly benefits and everyone gets the message that we want ideas.

Because the prizes are small and there are no complex criteria to assess, we can award them immediately. I have come across other companies' suggestion schemes where people wait for months or years to hear if their suggestion has been accepted. Needless to say, there is little incentive for people to contribute if they think it will be months before anyone even looks at their idea. Sometimes these schemes pay large rewards, but only for a very few approved contributions. A suggestion scheme shouldn't be like the National Lottery: it should be a well-used, motivational scheme for generating ideas.

Some organisations claim to have a suggestion scheme but moan that staff are too apathetic to use it. I usually find the so-called scheme consists of a dusty box in a corner, into which you can put a suggestion form which has to be obtained from the admin department at six weeks' notice and completed in triplicate.

We make our suggestion scheme easy to use and constantly urge staff to use it. Every new recruit joining the company is given our "What can we do?" book - a large book of simple forms on which they can write their suggestions. We make it very clear we want them to use this. But we know people generate more ideas in a group, so we encourage branches and departments to meet after hours, usually in the pub, and have a brainstorming session to come up with suggestions. The rewards are shared among them and when we spot that a branch has been slow to come forward with ideas, we remind them to keep the suggestions coming.

If you are thinking that this can't be worth the effort, because surely few ideas are worth using, you are wrong. We find about one in five ideas is worthy of further consideration, but the rest are not a waste of time. By seeing colleagues' suggestions I am learning what is happening on the shop floor and constantly scrutinising what we do. On consideration, there may be a good reason why we cannot implement a particular suggestion, but at least we will have examined it and asked the questions.

The leader must take charge of the suggestion scheme. This is a job I would not delegate to anyone else. For a start, it gives the scheme credibility. Staff know that I see their suggestions personally, so they know the scheme is not just an empty gesture.

It is also up to the leader to see that good ideas are implemented and do not just run into the sand at middle management level. This is especially true when hard-pressed directors are expected to action ideas that will involve them in more work. When a suggestion comes from me to another board member, it has far more impact than if it comes from a suggestion scheme manager lower down the organisation. When I want an improvement made, people know it's a priority. They had better not sit on it.

The suggestion scheme is a lot of work, but important. You will need to be ruthless about finding time to go through the suggestions. I might be reading a pile of 200 suggestions at 7 am on the train on the way to a meeting. I will start off reluctant to wade through them all, but once I start reading I am amazed by the valuable stuff that is in there. I am the first filter for suggestions and a very effective one. I know the business better than anyone, so if there's a nugget of a good idea I will spot it straight away.

Very soon those 200 ideas will be flying round the business. Some suggestions I can respond to myself, others need the involvement of other colleagues. I will pass certain suggestions on to David Robinson for comment, action and reward. Often I specifically ask for his feedback because the suggestions are so important I don't want them to be overlooked.

Other suggestions' I will decide to take to one of the meetings I chair – the design group, buyers meeting, catalogue planning meeting, or "What Hi-Fi?" planning meeting. As I'm going through the suggestions I mark them with the initial of the relevant group.

So at the beginning of the meeting I have a wad of suggestions to read out and we discuss them together. We usually get through at least 20 at the start of each meeting – our discussions are swift and to the point, we note the response and I decide then and there what reward to give for each suggestion.

The suggestion scheme is invaluable for making people feel involved in new initiatives. For example, when we introduced the EPOS system into Richer Sounds branches, it prompted a flood of suggestions. Could the new system do this? Why doesn't it do that? Our staff are not computer specialists, so it was right for them to ask the computer experts and challenge them. We found out how staff wanted to use the EPOS system and they felt involved in developing and improving it, instead of feeling it was simply imposed on them. Rather than their being slaves to the computer – as often happens – they made it their slave.

As the group of companies has grown, the suggestion scheme has become increasingly important. It keeps the contact between individual members of staff and myself. It is also an excellent way to bring people who have just joined the company into our culture. Within a few weeks, they can have put in a few suggestions and earned £100 tax free. Instantly, they are encouraged to think of more ideas.

When I say the chief must front the suggestion scheme, I often hear objections from people in other companies. "What if I know nothing about the area of work the suggestion covers?" The answer is obvious: bring in the expertise of your senior managers.

"It will take too long". It doesn't have to if you are decisive and work on the principles of a simple scheme, straightforward consideration and a large number of small rewards.

"It will mean extra work". Chiefs who raise this objection have completely missed the point. These ideas make your job easier, not harder. Every year I am astonished how many great ideas come out of the scheme – there are always diamonds to be found in there. And it's good to know my people are constantly thinking about the business and involved in moving it forward. That is kai zen.

Chapter 8

The value of people

When I am interviewed by the press, I am often asked, what is the secret of my success? I say it's simple - I have good people who work hard for the company.

I am sure everyone working in every organisation across the land has heard their chairman or chief executive go on about people being the most important asset of the business. Usually the chief has given very little thought to what this means and consequently, staff are cynical. But I do mean it when I say my business would be nothing without the people in it. The difference between me and most other leaders is that I am prepared to face up to the implications of that.

Many leaders are very remote from the workforce, either because they have worked their way up and have lost touch with their roots, or else because they have come in at the top and only have contact with the uppermost layers of management. The rest of the staff are lumped together and probably seen more as an overhead than an asset.

But to get real value out of your people you have to remember they are individuals, from the receptionist who's just joined to the warehouseman who's been there 20 years. If you remember they are individuals, with their own strengths and weaknesses, you can ensure that the business gets the maximum from them, by building on their strengths and managing their weaknesses.

You may be thinking that, as leader, surely this is not your job. You have managers to manage people. You are far too busy to be concerned about individuals.

This is the wrong attitude. It is the leader above all who should be aware of the workforce as people. It is your job to respond to them as individuals – which is exactly what I do when I make myself available for career counselling. It is your job to communicate with them, motivate them and see that they are being properly managed. You determine the overall management approach.

Of course dealing with people is time consuming. It can be a hassle, because people get stroppy or bring problems that can't be solved. But the payback is huge. Think of a business with 100 staff, undervalued and demotivated, some doing jobs they can't handle and others doing tasks they could carry out standing on their head. You are probably looking at an organisation working at 50% of its potential. Then think of those 100 people working at full capacity, in jobs that suit their skills and intelligence, enjoying the work and feeling rewarded for their efforts. It is obvious what a commercial advantage that company would then have.

Clearly in the real world there are no perfect employees, always perfectly happy and working flat out from nine 'til five. If there are any such paragons they haven't yet applied for a job with Richer Sounds, so in the meantime I have to make do with normal people. But I do work hard at ensuring I get the most out of those "normal" people.

There are four stages to getting the most out of your people:
- appointing the right people
- giving them the right things to do
- following up what they've done
- developing them.

If you can get these four stages right, you will be able to delegate properly, which is the key to good leadership. After all, employing people is only the first part of delegation. You cannot do everything yourself: you might start off doing it all, but in the end you cannot do the bookkeeping, serve the customers, write the adverts and answer the phones yourself. That is why you employ people and that is why you must care about who is employed and how they are managed.

Appointing the right people

Who are the right people? And how do you find them?

To find them, you have to know what you are looking for. I don't look for exceptional people. I'd rather have ordinary people who are exceptionally dedicated.

The qualities we value in my company are loyalty and integrity and, in my experience, you are more likely to find these qualities in ordinary people than in super-talented whizz kids. They know they don't need to work hard, so they're grasshoppers, flitting from one job to another. As soon as they've done you the honour of joining your company, they'll hop to a rival firm for more money.

It's very easy for bosses to play safe and hire the people who look good on paper, who've been to the right schools and the right university. Unfortunately, everyone else will be impressed with the CV too and they can choose the highest bidder.

The real test of your abilities as an employer is if you can look at an apparently "ordinary" person and see their potential. You have to look beyond the CV at the personality and their readiness to work hard. I find very often it's the people who have had a rather tougher time in the jobs market who show consistent, dedicated performance.

My company has many examples of exceptional talent and loyalty. The Group Managing Director, David Robinson, actually joined us as a 16 year old sales assistant. Many others who started out in relatively junior jobs, as sales assistants or in the warehouse, have really blossomed into dedicated colleagues who are a real asset to the business. We look for potential and don't assume that, just because someone is doing a manual job, they can never move into management. We've had people start in the warehouse who have gone on to be accountants. Our property manager, who also runs the Chelsea store, started in the warehouse.

When we take on young people, we like to make sure they are serious about the job and view it as a career, not just a way of filling in time until they get a "proper job". So we steer clear of rich kids and PhDs. I would rather take someone who may not have brilliant academic qualifications, but is enthusiastic about the job. There are a lot of young people out there in need of good jobs and I want to take on someone who hasn't had many opportunities and give them a break. We can develop them and they appreciate the chance they are given.

Apart from a few specialist posts, for example on the financial side, I find academic and professional qualifications matter much less than is generally thought. It is the qualities of the individual that really count and the qualities I look for are integrity, friendliness, enthusiasm and common sense. It is also important that you like the person and feel good about the prospect of working with them.

Friendliness and enthusiasm are the basis of good customer service. When we recruit staff for the branches, we look for friendliness, not the ability to sell. We believe giving good customer service is more important than making a sale, but customers will also be more inclined to buy from a friendly person. Friendliness is easy to judge when you are interviewing and of course first impressions count here. The customer will also make judgments on their first impression of your staff.

Formal qualifications do not matter as much as the ability and willingness to learn. Your managers will be teaching the new recruit the skills he or she needs. So they must be enthusiastic and ready to learn, but they must also have enough common sense to be able to learn.

If you are the leader of a large organisation you will probably not be involved with appointing junior staff. But it is still vitally important for you to have an interest in who is appointed and how, because those junior staff are the future of the business. They are also most likely to be the ones dealing with customers, so they are the public face of your company. Even if you are not hiring new staff yourself, you must set the criteria for senior managers who are doing the recruiting. Managers must be clear what your priorities are when taking on new staff.

You will certainly be involved in appointing senior managers. With luck, the people in the top posts will have come up through the organisation, so you will have a good idea of their qualities and capabilities. But if you are recruiting from outside, even at senior level, I would say the attributes you are looking for are not very different from those for juniors. Common sense is essential for senior people too – and their seniority is no guarantee that they possess it. They must have enthusiasm, or determination to see things through. Integrity is even more important at senior level than for juniors, because of the responsibilities they have and the example they must set to their staff.

You also have to like the person. This sounds subjective and maybe a little unprofessional, but it is important. If I see two job applicants with similar qualifications, I'll pick the person I like best. This is probably based on an irrational judgment, but when you're looking for people to be working around you, you must get on with them. If not, it's hard work.

So a person might not have exactly the qualifications you are looking for, but if they have potential and you get on well with them, you can get over most obstacles. I once made a mistake of promoting an unpopular man to a job. Everyone disliked working with him but I was reluctant to remove him as he had so much determination and was a great salesman. But in the end I realised he was more trouble than he was worth. People must get on with their colleagues and though he tried hard to please me, because I'm the boss, he caused endless upset with other people.

Subjective impressions do matter because everyone has to work with other people – customers and suppliers as well as colleagues within the organisation. If you don't like that person there's a good chance others won't. They could be creating bad feeling with your customers and suppliers.

Giving them the right things to do

My job as a leader is to get the most out of everybody. I want to get real value out of my people and the best way to do this is by giving them the things they're best at doing.

It's about efficiency. To get the most out of an engine, you have to design efficiency into it. To get the most out of an organisation, you have to ensure that each task is being done by the best person for the job.

Selecting the right person for the job is rarely recognised as a leadership skill, but it is hugely important. I would say being able to pick your people goes hand in hand with determination as the key to successful leadership.

How do you do it? You have to do the groundwork. You must observe your people, ask questions, see what they do well and what they can't get to grips with, think about how to use their strengths. You must be constantly looking at people with a critical eye. This doesn't mean constantly finding fault: it is as important to know people's strengths as their failings, because the strengths are what you can use.

I could go through the list of my directors and identify all their strengths and weaknesses. It is not disastrous if they have weaknesses - you just need to be aware of those so you can work round them. It is no use looking for the ideal director and be forever firing people because they're not perfect. Find out what the person is really good at and give them jobs which make use of those skills. If there are aspects of the job which they handle less well, pass those tasks on to someone else who can do them.

It is very important to get this right with the 10 people around you. You personally can only do so much work in a day, make so many phone calls and have so many meetings. To work with maximum impact you need to delegate to your 10 key people and those 10 have to be good. They absolutely must be the right people in the right positions: they must be inspired, motivated, and have the ability to do what you want them to do.

With your 10 people around you, you must make sure you give each task that comes up to the right person.

The right person is not always obvious at first sight and you do have to try people out. One important question to ask is, what are the essential skills for this job? Again, it is not always the skills you first think of.

Most people would say a marketing director needs to be creative, but should that be their most important attribute? Our marketing director, who worked her way up from a junior post, is excellent. But she is a good manager, not an airy-fairy arty type. She manages a budget of £1 million a year and runs a department providing marketing services to 10 companies, plus several charities.

My decision to appoint her as marketing director proved to be the right one. The leader must be able to spot people's potential. You must be able to see, not just what they do now but what they could do in future if they were developed.

You also have to be firm about what they cannot do. Never be distracted by someone's length of service or how hard they work. It is not good thinking someone "deserves" promotion because they are so dedicated. You have to stick with your decision that someone is a good sales assistant but they will not make a manager. If you can't promote them, you must find other ways to motivate them and make clear they are valued. But when you have assessed a person's strengths and weaknesses, you should stick by your judgment.

There is undoubtedly a lot of trial and error involved. Lower down the organisation, this is not necessarily a bad thing. At Richer Sounds, we are quick to promote, quick to demote. We are not afraid to try people out in a new job, on the understanding that if they are not up to it, they will return to their old job with no shame involved. You might think people will leave if they are demoted, but we find that is rarely the case. Often people are relieved to be removed from a job they couldn't handle.

That even applies to more senior managers. You don't really know who will be a good manager until they are in the job. Our managers are all very different. Broadly, some are good administrators, good with procedures and others are good with people. But both types can be excellent managers. Don't have a blinkered definition of what makes a good manager.

Appointing people to very senior positions, such as heading a subsidiary company, is much more risky. You cannot afford too much experimentation. People must be given a chance, but clearly you have to move swiftly if their poor performance is damaging the company. My success rate with these kind of appointments is probably best when entrepreneurial people come to me from outside and want my help in setting up a business. They are usually dedicated and highly motivated with a good grasp of the responsibilities. But with some notable exceptions, it has proved more difficult to take people out of the security of Richer Sounds and give them their own business to run.

So this ability to select people is vital for a leader. I tended to view people critically even at a young age, having a few close friends rather than a big gang. I'm still like that in my social life. I have many friends but I hate going out with 30 people to some chaotic restaurant where you end up yelling at each other about nothing. I'd much rather have a dinner for four and some intelligent conversation.

I am interested in people. When I meet staff, I think about where I would position them in the group. That's why I'm happy doing career counselling. For example, I saw a young woman who used to work for Richer Sounds but left to study electronic engineering. She asked to see me with a view to her rejoining the company. In a 10 minute chat I immediately thought of three places she could go in the company.

There is a skill there that you can develop. With experience, you will become more confident at taking decisions about people and more of your decisions will be the right ones.

This skill is completely different from being "a people person". Being nice and sociable is not what it's about. Individuals who are intent on being liked often make rotten managers because they spend all day chatting and have no discipline.

You do have to be good with people in the sense that you must be able to communicate and get people to do what you want. All the time that you are chairing meetings, giving seminars and representing the company to the outside world, you will need these skills. But you also have to be good at analysing the figures and reading reports.

Following up and developing people
These two are closely linked. As I explained in Chapter 3, following up is a necessary part of delegating. You can't just give people work and forget about it. They must report back to you, at a set time which is entered on to

your worksheet.

When you follow up, not only are you ensuring that the task was done but you also assess how it was done and whether it was done on time. Did the person handle it well or were they struggling? How did they cope with obstacles? Did they use their initiative or come back to you for instructions?

To follow up, you must give feedback, or else people will not develop. It is the leader's job to coach people, so that next time they do the job better.

People won't come to work for you ready formed. No-one is born with experience. They have to be given the benefit of the communal experience of the organisation. They should be learning all the time, through a number of routes. There are training events, like seminars, but there are many ways each day that people learn, through feedback and communications from you, through being given new tasks. If you have continuous improvement in your organisation, you should also have continuous development for your people.

A lot of learning is via mistakes. Some leaders put this forward as a reason not to delegate: they think there will be fewer mistakes if they do everything themselves. But this is a poor argument. For a start, your people will never develop unless they are allowed to do things on their own, and inevitably they will sometimes make mistakes.

A few years ago, I found a marvellous way to develop my people - by accident. I decided I wanted to work less, in order to take stock, so I started taking alternate weeks out of the office. I put myself out of reach of work, only phoning in once a day and never leaving my mobile on.

At first I was very nervous and kept asking people what it was like when I wasn't there. They assured me it was fine and they appreciated the chance to get on with their work while I was not around. Then I realised that, without me on their backs, they made a quantum leap in development. They were making more decisions for themselves. They saw me only one week in two so they had to learn how to bring only the essentials to me.

The result showed in the figures. I had the best of both worlds: the profits shot up and I had a lot more time on my hands to pursue other commercial interests. Many people with their own business are terrified of going on holiday in case the company falls apart. But I found the more I distanced myself, the stronger it got. A business must have self-sufficiency. It will be worth little if potential buyers look at it and see it cannot operate without you.

Distancing yourself is fine, but you must also have the systems in place to spot any failures before they go too far. With your layers of 10 in place, and people regularly reporting back to you, you can limit the scope of their mistakes. You have to make sure that the key information - for example, how far a budget has been spent - comes back to you.

You also have to create a culture of openness, so that people are prepared to admit they've screwed up. Many people's instinct when they make a mistake is to hide it under the carpet. If their boss threatens to fire them as soon as things go wrong, they will go to great lengths to cover up. This applies to senior managers as well as junior staff - and the danger is that senior managers' mistakes are usually much more expensive. As leader, you must ensure that people are ready to come to you when they have a problem. I might rant and rave a bit when things go wrong, but I am much more angry if I find I haven't been told about a mistake. Once I've stopped shouting, I'm ready to work with that person to sort out the problem. With luck, they will learn and next time will be able to sort it out on their own.

People don't like telling me about their mistakes, of course, but they know it's better for them to come to me, take a deep breath and deliver the bad news, than for me to find out they haven't told me.

We insist that in their Friday night reports to me, people must put the bad news at the top. If you have bad news, you've got to get that off your chest first. I am in the position of a General commanding from the hilltop: I need a clear view of what's happening on the field and if I'm not told bad news, I do not have that view. Once I've heard the problems, I can draw on all my experience and expertise to deal with them.

Developing people is an essential leadership role. If you are a good leader, people will listen to you more than to anyone else. You have most to offer them, both through instilling in them the values and priorities of the organisation, and through the power to make them feel valued. Developing your people is about being available and accessible for them. It is about giving them recognition, meeting their aspirations instead of making them plead with you for a pay rise every year. If you are developing people well, they will be loyal. I have some excellent managers and directors. There's nothing they like better than casually mentioning they've been contacted by a headhunter offering them double their salary - they know it winds me up! But they have no intention of leaving (I hope!).

Motivation

In my book "The Richer Way", I explained why so many organisations give poor customer service. It's because they do not manage their staff properly: they fail to motivate them and staff who do not feel valued will not value the customer.

Few people turn up to work each morning for the sheer joy of it - they need to be motivated. They need to be rewarded, not just financially, as many bosses mistakenly believe, but also in terms of enjoyment and respect. As the leader, it is your job to ensure this motivation is there.

Each individual will be motivated by a combination of different factors, but motivation does not have to be left to chance. It is possible to take a systematic approach, with five steps to motivation.

I. Fun

I believe a job should be as much fun as possible. If you enjoy what you do, you will do it better. So the leader should be thinking of ways to inject some fun into the business. Richer Sounds is well known for the things we do: a string of holiday homes for staff and their family and friends, the chance for branches which come top in customer service each month to swank around in a Rolls-Royce.

Fun also means banning long hours, six day weeks and macho, workaholic attitudes. We want our staff relaxed and ready to put all their energy into serving the customer.

The important thing about fun is that it needs fresh ideas. People still enjoy the luxury cars and the holiday homes, but the novelty always wears off. To keep the impact, I want to surprise and delight them every year with new ideas so I put a lot of thought into what we can do next.

2. Recognition

One of the most powerful motivational tools you possess is a simple "thank you". How often do your staff get thanked for a job well done? If their manager thanks them, they will be pleased, but if it comes from the chief executive or chair the message will be twice as powerful.

It is very easy to ring someone up or send a note to say "thank you", but we rarely do it unless we build recognition into the system. Letters can be a chore, but it is important to do them and do them straight away. Enter it on your worksheet. When I visit one of our branches and it looked good, I write and tell them so afterwards. I have seen these letters pinned up on staff notice boards years later, still a source of pride.

Recognition needs to be systematic, so that it is consistent and not just at your whim. We have recognition schemes open to everyone, such as our gold aeroplane badges for "high flyers" who have excelled in customer service.

Every Sunday night, I call the Richer Sounds branches which have done well and leave a message of congratulations on their answerphone. For 19 years I used to call every branch myself on a Monday morning, but as the group has grown, I no longer have the time and now the managing director or deputy managing director does those calls. But even my quick answerphone messages have an impact: the branches often say it gives them a boost to hear me saying "well done" first thing on a Monday.

These are small gestures, but together they can build up into an organisational culture which is always ready to recognise good work. The best way to create this culture is for you to start it from the top.

3. Rewards

People should be rewarded fairly and in my company we pay good wages for our industry. The two important principles are: firstly, that people should be able to be rewarded for working better, and secondly that the business should reward what it values.

Flat salaries are demotivating. It is better to institute some form of reward scheme, preferably several schemes, by which your staff can earn more for good performance, and that includes secretaries and warehouse staff as well as staff in the shops.

What you reward will be what gets done, so what do you want your business to achieve? In my company we want to give the customer great service, so staff are rewarded for giving great service. Many businesses say customer service is important to them, but in fact their rewards are based on profits, turnover or market share. Their staff know they will get commission on a sale, regardless of whether the customer went away happy or not.

Our sales staff have a low basic salary, supplemented by a number of reward schemes. A larger proportion of a staff member's salary is earned through customer service bonuses, profit sharing and other incentives such as the suggestion scheme, than through sales commission.

It is best to have a number of reward schemes, applying to as many people as possible. You can reward any aspect of the work you want, provided you measure it properly. I am often told by other companies that good service is "too subjective" to measure and reward, but my book "The Richer Way" explains exactly how we measure the quality of service given by our staff and how we reward accordingly. For the scheme to be meaningful, there must also be penalties if the customer was not happy with the service.

Profit share is also a good motivator, if you reward little and often and in a way that everyone can see is fair. Profit share should not be confined to the leader and top directors, although for the top layer of management it should form a more important part of their remuneration. Their responsibility is that much greater, so they can win more by the business doing well, but they should also take more of the pain when things go badly.

We now have a weekly profit share in the branches. Colleagues at the support office receive their profit share once every four months. But in the shops we have devised a do-it-yourself sharing scheme.

Every Saturday night after the shop closes, each branch works out its own profit, using the gross profit figures from the EPOS system, the fixed costs supplied by the central office and their own variable costs, such as casual labour, local advertisements and petty cash. They fill in the boxes and instantly know how much profit they've made. Every week 7% of that profit is for them to share between all the staff who have been with the company three months or more. We recommend the manager gets five times as much as the non-management, though they can alter that ratio if they want. Some branch managers have chosen to share it out equally.

Those 52 profit shares a year generate a great sense of involvement with the business. Everyone has a stake in the week to week performance of their branch.

4. Communication

You cannot motivate your workforce unless you communicate with them. I don't just mean issuing orders: I mean explaining what the mission and strategy of the business is, telling them what you expect of them and how they are measuring up, informing them about the company's progress.

There are many ways to communicate from the top directly to staff, through talks and seminars, videos, phone calls and so on. The leader should be out there communicating, not closeted in the board room day after day.

Another way to communicate is simply to go and talk to people. This is often called Management By Walking Around and it is one of those things most leaders would like to do but few get round to. The only way to ensure you do it is to schedule an MBWA hour or two hours in your diary. Two hours direct communication with your staff every month should not be out of the question, and you will find it hugely productive, in terms of both motivation and valuable information for yourself.

I schedule visits to the warehouse and the central departments like accounts and marketing. I try to talk to every single person, albeit briefly, and it takes a couple of hours. I normally ask people three things: Are you happy? Are there any problems? Is there anything you want to tell me?

I remember one of our employees at the warehouse being asked by a journalist, what he thought was special about working at Richer Sounds? He didn't mention the Rolls Royces or the holiday homes or the money. He said it was the fact that he could talk to the Chairman. MBWA is really one of the smallest things I do but it has a powerful impact.

As your business gets bigger, walking around becomes even more important. It is completely different to all the other communications you have with people. I always take notes and come back with a lot of information about what is happening outside my office, how people are working and problems they raise.

When I have noted things to do, however small, I make a real point of following through. If someone in accounts tells me they have an uncomfortable chair, I go back and make sure it is replaced. It is a minor thing but they will always remember that the Chairman listened to their complaint and sorted it out.

I once visited our sub-contractor's distribution warehouse at Christmas and found people putting plugs on CD players in the freezing cold. I asked them if they needed anything, like warm clothes and they said they were due to get some soon, so I made a note to check up on that. Then one said, "some music would be nice". So I took him seriously, and back in the car, phoned the nearest Richer Sounds branch and asked them to install some hi-fi in the warehouse that afternoon. The warehouse workers will probably tell that story for the rest of their lives.

It could have taken a month to put that hi-fi in, but it was the same amount of work to do it instantly and it had a huge impact. It was a gesture that showed I was listening. People do not expect that from the chairman or chief executives – they expect you to be too busy to care. So if you can demonstrate that you do listen, with some caring gestures, that will go a long way.

Communication must be from the bottom up as well as top down. There is little point in going around talking to people unless you are prepared to listen to what they say and act upon it. You might not always like what you hear, but it is still crucial information. If all you hear is complaints, either you are hiring a lot of miserable people or there is a motivation problem.

You need to set up systems for upwards communication. We have various ways of listening to people's ideas, views and problems, such as the suggestion scheme, "Question Time" at seminars and training sessions, career counselling and so on. These are valuable safety valves. In a tightly controlled business like mine, people must have safety valves, so that we find out early on if procedures aren't working or there is resentment building up among staff. Then we can act before a problem grows too large.

We take a very tough line on whingeing. We have a lot of small teams out in the branches: they enjoy substantial benefits but we push them hard. There is nothing more negative than permanent moaners. They have a corrosive effect on their co-workers in the branch or in the department, dragging down morale and therefore business.

So we make it clear right from the start that we will not tolerate whingers. They will be out of a job. The reason we can adopt such a dictatorial approach in terms of people's civil right to moan is that they can whinge as much as they like when they go home, but in the workplace it is unnecessary, as we have many upwards communication safety valves for them to give vent to their dissatisfaction.

5. Loyalty

If you want loyalty from your people – and most leaders do – you must demonstrate it in return. Loyalty is a powerful motivator. Again, you want a range of measures that demonstrate in practice that you care about your staff. At Richer Sounds we put 1% of our profits into a hardship fund, to provide grants or interest-free loans for staff who are in difficulties, for example if a partner is made redundant and they have sudden financial problems. We have never known staff to abuse this fund. We have a subsidised healthcare scheme, but if someone is ill and is not happy with their GP, we will also pay for them to see my doctor on Harley Street. This is another of those small gestures that sends a powerful message.

To the leader, juggling weighty decisions, employees' concerns can seem trivial. But when staff come to you with apparently small problems, you must take them seriously. My housemaster at school, Ernest Polack, who was a big influence on me, worked for a while on a teacher exchange in a borstal. He said the kids there had the most terrible problems, often telling him of awful abuse or violence in the family. He then came back to this namby pamby public school and the worst problem the boys brought to him was that they had lost their pocket money or someone had moved their football boots. But these boys were just as anxious and he took their problems just as seriously, because he knew it was all relative.

So don't dismiss a person's complaint that their computer is too slow, just because you have got bigger things like the overdraft to worry about. People's small worries can snowball into big resentments. Your business's biggest asset goes home every night and the last thing you want is for it to not come back again in the morning but be off to another company.

Leadership is about relationships, which means you must make sure the channels of communication are open between you and every person in the organisation. Most of the time, they will be getting on with their jobs, but you must be confident that, if anything goes wrong, the person will be willing to come to you so you can act before the problem snowballs. It is up to you to create that relationship and that approachability.

The payback

Even if you do manage to walk around the office once a month, it is impossible for you know how everyone in the company feels about their job. But you can easily measure motivation levels in the business via a few simple indicators. This should be part of the information that is constantly being fed back to you. Once you look at these indicators, the payback on treating your people well becomes strikingly clear.

Labour turnover is one yardstick to measure people's satisfaction with the job. It is a crude measure, because if labour turnover is low, it doesn't necessarily mean people are happy - it could just be that there are few other jobs locally. But if it is high relative to your industry you can definitely take it that something is wrong. At Richer Sounds we push staff hard, so we don't count the recruits that leave within a few weeks because they can't take the pace. But once people stay and become valued and experienced members of staff, we are concerned if they leave.

High absentee rates are a sure sign of demotivated staff. If you treat your staff well and they are happy working for you, they will take fewer days off sick. I know that because the national absenteeism rate is 4-5% and in my company the rate is 1-2%.

Fraud and "shrinkage", as we in the retail trade call staff theft, also indicate problems. Your procedures may be lax, but it may also be that staff are resentful. People often cheat on their employers if they feel their employers are cheating on them, for example if they have to work long hours without overtime.

Customer satisfaction is also a measure of staff motivation. You need keen staff in order to give your customers good service. I can bet that if you have a branch or department where customer complaints are high, its absenteeism rate, labour turnover and shrinkage will also be high. There are staff - or rather management - problems there that you must sort out.

Every year at Richer Sounds we also measure staff motivation specifically via an attitude survey. This is carried out in full confidentiality, and staff trust that confidentiality so, we believe, they give honest replies to a list of questions on how they feel about the job. An attitude survey will give the leader much food for thought - your staff will often tell you things you might not want to hear. A survey should never be a one off: the point is to repeat it so that each year you can see if the business is doing better at motivating its staff.

There is a big payback to all of this because high labour turnover, absenteeism and shrinkage all cost money. Poor customer service costs you even more money and the worst part is that you will never know how much it has cost you. Bear in mind that the text books say every dissatisfied customer tells up to 20 other people about the poor service they received, but only one unhappy customer in 20 complains directly to the company.

So for every complaint you receive, there could be 19 other people complaining about you to their friends – each telling 20 others! That is costing you a lot of business. That is why my company does everything possible to encourage customer complaints! At first it may look as if we have a lot of unsatisfied customers, but I would rather they came to us so that we can put the problem right and, we hope, turn an unhappy customer into a happy one.

So the accountants will tell you the company cannot possibly afford holiday homes and birthday cards for the staff. But it is your job as leader to look beyond those costs, to the payback. You have to take care of your people: it is up to you as the chief to stand up for your staff against the bean counters. Accountants do a good job and you need them, but you must be the one that keeps things in perspective and recognises the true worth of well-motivated staff and satisfied customers.

The role model

If you are a good leader, you will have a strong influence over your staff. You may not know all of them individually but remember they all know who you are. It is important to use this influence wisely.

As leader, you have the power to create a climate of equality and openness in the workplace. Racism, sexism, bullying and other abuses should never be allowed to flourish. Inevitably, people have different views on this, some people crack jokes without realising they offend others and so on. But in a civilised workplace lines need to be drawn, and you are the person to draw them. As a leader you should look at the highest common denominator not the lowest. There will be things that you do not find offensive but if you see they upset others, you have to take a stand against them. I admit I'm terrible at swearing and I do have to be careful there, as things I might say without thinking could offend other people. In fact most people are very uncomfortable with their boss swearing in front of them, no matter what kind of language they might use at home.

You have to make a statement about what is and is not acceptable. People will then take their cue from you. At the "virgin" seminar for new recruits I always tell them we do not tolerate any form of prejudice or harassment, so they know from the start.

I think racism is easy to spot, but sexism is often harder to judge, especially since the workforce in my company is predominantly male. The best thing is to have a climate of openness where female staff feel confident about complaining about sexist language.

When I took over as chairman of Tecno, a chain selling photographic equipment, I noticed its warehouse had topless girly pictures all over the walls. One look at most photographic magazines will tell you this is part of the culture of this industry. I'm not a puritan but I found it unacceptable as I thought it would intimidate the female workforce. So the message went round all the Tecno shops and offices to take down the girly pictures. I wanted to stamp my own culture on the company from day one.

Once you set the standards, you must stick to them yourself. People pick up very quickly on any kind of hypocrisy. The essential job for the leader is to put all these principles into action. My five steps to motivation are totally practical – it is no good talking about them, you have to do them. It is no good announcing you are going to introduce "fun" into the company and the next day sending out a memo ordering staff not to waste paper clips. Your job is to lead people, not patronise them.

Chapter 9

Key people

Every person in your organisation is important, but there is a group of people who are particularly important to you in your job as leader. These are the 10 people who report directly to you and to whom you delegate.

If you have 10 or so good people here, you can achieve a great deal. It might be a dozen, but you shouldn't have more than 15 people reporting directly to you as you will not be able to monitor and develop them properly, as well as doing your own job.

So who are your key people? They might be your managing director, MDs of subsidiary organisations, senior directors such as finance, marketing, personnel, customer services, your secretary or personal assistant, then perhaps others such as non executive directors.

With 10 people, each of whom has 10 people reporting to them and so on, you can quickly command a large army.

Your time is limited, so don't have people reporting to you if you never have time to see them. If they only get the chance to see you personally twice a year, it is demotivating for them and they will not be working at their best. Ten key people is enough to maintain a business working efficiently. This is one good reason for keeping the structure of your company simple and having no more departments than is necessary.

My 10 people are hand-picked and most have been working with me for many years. Working close to me is not a cushy number: I push people hard because I want them to do things to the quality I demand. My job is to delegate the work, set those high standards and follow up. I find that they do rise to the challenge – in fact they relish it. If people are good, they don't mind being pushed hard as long as they get due recognition.

When I say they must do things to the quality I would do them, I don't mean they have to do everything in the same way as I would. They all have their own style. I often pick people who are very different in temperament to myself – I don't always want to be surrounded by people as manic as me! This is especially true for board members.

The board

A balance of personalities is very important for your company board. You don't need a large board, as long as all the members contribute something. Our group board has only four members: myself and three others.

I drive the board meetings and at a typical meeting I probably do 90% of the talking. So I admit the others have to be good listeners. But I do listen to what they say, and what they say does count.

The other three board members are the group managing director, who is responsible for about 10 different divisions, the finance director for the group, and the managing director of our manufacturing business.

The group MD is the person to whom I delegate most. He is a first class professional manager and excellent at getting things done. He is particularly good at all the jobs I hate, like contracts, insurance and litigation (though, thankfully, there is not much of the latter). He regards them as a challenge. Wacky entrepreneurs like me get bored with all the dry, legal stuff, but it is very important to have at least one person around who can deal with that, because these are issues which can cost – or save – your business large sums of money.

The head of manufacturing is on the board because he is so shrewd. He is not only a good manager but has an exceptionally sharp brain and is a great strategist. I can bring a complicated problem to the board and he is on to it straight away with an amazing problem-solving mind. He and I also talk the same language, commercially. But again, he is very different to me - quiet and thoughtful. He is always trying to do everything a better way, which is invaluable for the business.

I do the inspirational entrepreneur stuff, investigating new business ideas, jetting off to Nice to look at a yacht for the company, and they let me get on with it. They know if I want to buy a yacht for the staff, I'll have to prove to them it would be worth it, but they also know they've got to give me a bit of space. Incidentally, we decided the yacht would not be a good investment because of the huge running costs, but are looking at new holiday homes.

I also give them plenty of space. I normally see them once a month and in between meetings I'm not on their backs all the time. I don't phone them to find out where they are, what time they get into the office in the morning, how many days they've worked. I'm not constantly hassling them to find out how they're getting on with the work I've delegated to them. In a month's time we will have a meeting and they will have to report back to me on what they've done. The focus is on delivering results rather than the number of hours spent slogging away.

When you are deciding who should be on your board, you should seek a balance of skills and personalities. Particularly look for people who have strengths that counterbalance your own weaknesses. You need people who are intelligent, articulate and numerate. A quick grasp of figures is essential for the people who are running the business. We in fact call our meetings financial review meetings rather than board meetings. This puts the focus firmly on probably the most important issue: the financial health of the business.

Personal assistants

Good secretaries and PAs are very important for a leader. A good PA can save you an unbelievable amount of time, freeing you up for the important tasks. Good chief executives have good PAs, so they can get through the volume of work. Without doubt, the efficiency of my two assistants, Christine Nelson and Teresa Chapman, enables me to do all the different things I've chosen to do.

A PA should screen calls for you, keep your diary, make travel arrangements and prepare letters. MDs are idiots if they write their own letters, other than handwritten courtesy notes. An experienced PA can draft standard letters or work from your notes or a memo recorder, and all you have to do is sign.

Christine, my PA, plays a valuable role as my eyes and ears to the outside world. As well as handling my correspondence, including letters from customers, she frequently deals with customers on the phone. This is a skilled job, especially if there has been a major blunder and an unhappy customer is ranting and raving about the company. She has to mollify the customer, but also protect me, because although I always deal with complaints from customers, I never do it over the phone. Christine will handle them on my behalf and if they demand a reply from me, she suggests they write to me so that I can respond.

Christine has also taken on other tasks over the years. She has about 10 people reporting to her, such as the housekeepers of the holiday homes, the receptionists and other office personnel.

My productivity has gone up hugely since I have had a full time diary secretary. I was spending what seemed like hours on the phone each week, simply arranging meetings. Now Teresa does all that: I decide whom to meet and she sorts out when and where. This is a time consuming job and it was a great release for me to be free of it. Where there are several people involved, or diaries are full, it can take hours to arrange a meeting.

Teresa also saves me time by screening out the people I don't want or need to see and by minimising meetings. Someone might ask to meet me for dinner, but she will suggest instead early evening drinks, or a breakfast meeting. She arranges the day so that my time is used efficiently, with the least possible trouble in getting from one meeting to another.

To get good assistants, you have to pay them top money and motivate them. My assistants are fully involved with the business and frequently put in good suggestions. You also need to take them into your confidence. I have no problem with that as I am a very open person, but it is important as they will need your trust in order to do their job properly.

Reporting structure

The key to using your 10 people effectively is to have a sound reporting structure. This goes hand in hand with the worksheet, as I explained in chapter 5. To be able to delegate effectively, you must have people reporting back to you in a systematic way - but also let them get on with the job in the meantime.

On a Friday night I get reports in from my directors around the business. Some send in more than one report if they are responsible for several areas of business. They will all know where I am on a Friday night - whether at my home in York or in London - and they will fax the reports over. So each person reporting directly to me - that is, all the people on my worksheet - will send me one page of bullet points, telling me what they have achieved during the week, any problems, anything they want to ask me and so on.

I then have the weekend to go through the reports and I'm ready to get back to each director when I see them on a Monday afternoon. We blast through their report and sort out any problems. I go through their outstanding jobs and give them new work.

This means that I never go into a meeting without being prepared. I'm ready with questions about all the tasks I asked them to do last week and all the new things I want to delegate to them. That is how we can get through 11 meetings in one afternoon.

So Mondays are really hard work, but this frees up the rest of the week.

Once a week I have a structured meeting with Christine. Apart from that, I phone in to my secretaries once a day, wherever I may be, and they fax over my messages each evening. My message sheets are numbered, to ensure none are lost. I can't afford to miss out on urgent information like the time of a meeting being changed. If there are no messages, they send a fax to tell me so. If you are abroad and the only lifeline back to the office is your hotel fax, you cannot take any chances.

Although I push my key people hard, I'm not hassling them every day. After the meeting, they go away and get on with their work. As I have explained in chapter 5, about the way I manage my people, I am not constantly ringing up and loading more work on to them. But they know I will be checking up on them in a week's time, so they get things done. I try to tie people down: I never give people open-ended tasks, but always set a deadline. Of course, it will not always be possible to complete things by the deadline, but it puts a gentle pressure on people to deliver.

Chapter 10

Your tasks

So you have your 10 people around you, with a strong system of delegating and following up. That frees you to do the important tasks. But what are the true tasks of a leader? What cannot be delegated?

Deciding the strategy

Most leaders will recognise this as a fundamental role. Make sure you are not delegating this without realising it. The raw material of building a strategy is information and ideas. You should be constantly gathering this information yourself, not just relying on reports and advice from juniors.

You should be visiting and observing the competition, keeping abreast of new business formulas. You need to know what is happening in your market and what is just over the horizon - you can't come up with the strategy if you don't know what the hell's going on out there. This means doing the research, reading the newspapers and trade periodicals. I read the "Financial Times" every single day. It means finding out about new technology in your business, not leaving that to the technical experts.

Only with good and wide-ranging information can you develop a view of where the business should be heading at any one time.

Motivating

Clearly you have to motivate, develop and inspire your 10 people around you so they can then cascade it down through the organisation.

As leader you will also be motivating the rest of the workforce, in a less formal, but very influential, way.

You have to lead from the front. That sounds like a contradiction of the whole business of delegating, but it's not. It is about respect. People will respect a leader who does not ask them to do a job that the leader would never do himself or herself.

My staff know that I understand exactly what it is like working in a store because I have done it myself. There are things I haven't done much of, such as specialist work with computers (none!) or heavy labour in the warehouses (a little). But occasionally I make the gesture and people see me putting on a pair of dungarees and shifting boxes in the warehouse. That's what I mean by leading from the front and it's worth an enormous amount in terms of credibility.

It is easier for me as people know I built the business from nothing. But if you are heading a business that you did not create yourself, a few gestures are very important. You don't have to pitch in at the frontline all the time, but the occasional gesture can be powerful, provided you are genuinely willing to do that job properly. Staff will quickly see through you if you're not willing to get your hands dirty, literally or metaphorically.

Making decisions

As I said in chapter 3, you have to be a decision-making machine. People will be constantly coming to you for decisions. This is where you need to be sure that you are not the only decision-maker in the organisation, with managers delegating upwards to you. You should be delegating as much as you can - which means other people should be making their own decisions and reporting back to you.

Driving the business forward

You must be the power source for the business, its dynamo. This particularly applies when the organisation is going through difficult times or is on something of a plateau - you must keep pushing people forwards.

The leader must drive kai zen, through such mechanisms as the suggestion scheme. The point about continuous improvement is that everyone should be involved: everyone should be coming forward with ideas and the improvements that result must be applied consistently across the board. But without one person tirelessly demanding improvements, it will lose momentum. People will settle into doing things the same old way, unless you are there pushing for something better.

A hand on the tiller

Keeping in control is a key task for the leader. Your organisation should be like a spider's web, with you at the centre. Essential information should be fed back to you regularly through this network. The next chapter will look at how you should do this and what kind of information you need. This doesn't mean only keeping the long term goals in sight - it also comes down to watching the cash.

Being a figurehead for staff

I'm not into ego trips. I think it's a mistake to cultivate a high personal profile or let the media turn you into a celebrity figure. But however shy you are, you must be prepared to be identifiable and up-front for two important sets of people - your staff and your customers.

Being a figurehead means your staff should know who you are and what you stand for. In practice, you cannot be in daily touch with each member of staff, motivating them personally. But there will be no motivation if you are some distant, mythical figure they recognise only from a photo in the annual report.

A figurehead is something of a symbolic role and, although you must do some very practical things, a lot of it is achieved through key, symbolic gestures. When I say I will give career counselling I mean it, but in reality only a small number of staff will ever take up that offer. But as long as I demonstrate that I am genuinely ready to find 15 minutes to listen to

someone, the message will get through and staff will have confidence in me.
The effect of a small gesture spreads out like ripples in a pond.

To use your time for maximum effectiveness, you have to judge what are
the key moments for staff. What can you do that will have the greatest
impact on them?

One of those key moments is when they join the company. I go to our
"virgin" seminars to give new recruits that first push. Other managers then
take over the rest of the training. Properly organised, this can take less than a
day of my time. I will shoot up to our training centre at York, give an hour
long session which is a powerful burst of inspiration, and then, if time
permits, see each new staff member individually. They queue outside my
study and I see them for a couple of minutes each. I'm welcoming them to
the company but this is not an idle chat: I make notes on my impressions of
every one of them and go through those afterwards with the personnel
director.

When I ask managers the following week how their staff got on at the
virgin seminar, they always say the recruits were very impressed with me!
That's good - as a leader, it is your staff you should be impressing, not the
Sunday papers.

If you were in battle, short of ammunition, you would use your bullets
judiciously. Leaders are always short of time, so spread the personal contact
around for maximum impact.

The same reasoning lies behind my pre-Christmas visit to the branches.
I can only make one visit a year to every single one of them, so I make sure I
do it when it will have the greatest impact, just before our biggest season.
I can galvanise the branches into looking superb and giving top service, so
customers get maximum benefit.

Being a figurehead for customers

Your customers should know your name. They should even know what you look like. Our Richer Sounds catalogue always has a picture of me looking smiley and friendly, telling people to write to me if they have any comments or complaints about our products or the service they received in our shops. They certainly do write in - and not always to complain.

Many chiefs feel uncomfortable about identifying themselves to customers in this way. Maybe they feel it's a bit tacky and American, rather undignified. Perhaps they think it will be seen as a gigantic ego trip. But it is not: it is about facing your customers, saying, "Thank you for buying our products and paying our wages, and if there's anything you are not happy about, let me know". It is about taking responsibility. Many companies ask customers to write to some box number if they have a complaint, which is very impersonal and does not inspire confidence that the complaint will be dealt with. It means much more if you give people your name and say "I run this business. If we screw up, tell me".

It is important to have your picture there too. For a start, people can see you're a real human being and if you look friendly, you are making a good impression, just as your staff should be making a good impression by their friendliness. If you think a photo of you is more likely to scare the customers off, don't hesitate to use all the tricks of lighting, make-up and clever photography to come up with something flattering!

This will mean your image and the image of the company are inextricably linked. Again, some chiefs are uncomfortable with this. Some might not be planning to head their company for long before they move on elsewhere and do not want to tie themselves down. But that should not be an obstacle. Customers are usually buying for today - they won't necessarily remember your name unless they become very regular customers (or make a lot of complaints). A new managing director joining an organisation can make a selling point of it, telling customers "I'm in charge now - I want to hear from you".

You should be a figurehead, a focus to demonstrate that your business is accountable to its customers. People like to see a face: just as they would hate to be served in a shop by someone whose face they cannot see, they will warm to a business that does not present a blank, impersonal front to the world.

The point of doing this is to get customers to respond to you. As I've explained, if any customers are not satisfied, you want them to complain to you, not to their friends. It is vital to create safety valves, to make it easy for your customers to tell you what they think.

In my company we have these safety valves at every stage of the customer interface. On all our receipts there is a short, tear-off questionnaire, with just five questions. We ask them to send the replies to me, at a freepost address. If they don't buy anything but are given a quote, that form also invites them to write to me. If (even worse) they never got served, but left after standing in a queue, they can still pick up a 'We're Listening' card, prominently displayed on the counter, asking them for comments on the service they have (or haven't) received.

My name is always on these, because I do want to know if we are not giving a good service. But note that I ask people to write to me. At least one high-profile head of a company makes the mistake of asking customers to ring him if they haven't enjoyed the product or have any comments. I know a couple of people who've tried to phone him and of course he's never there. He is trying to appear accessible, but customers find out it's just bullshit.

So if you are going to make claims to customers, you have to be realistic and credible. If you invite comment you must make it easy for people to comment and you must reply. If you encourage people to complain, you must deal with the complaints or the company's reputation will suffer. Your personal reputation will suffer because you have put your name to it.

It is much easier to cope with letters from customers. People tend to rant on the phone, but if they have to sit down and write a letter, they calm down a little. If you are lucky, they will explain the complaint so that you can check out the facts.

I aim to be accessible to customers, but I make a point of never speaking to them on the phone. This is not a contradiction. If customers speak to you direct, they will expect some kind of instant response. But it is unfair to your staff to take the customer's side before you have had a chance to ask staff members for their record of events. I find customers rarely invent a complaint, but they often blow up a small problem into a large one.

On the whole, you should take the line that the customer is right. If someone feels they were made to wait an unreasonable amount of time to be served, that is a real perception that you must address. If you are serious about customer service, that means giving the customer the benefit of the doubt, even if sometimes they were being unreasonable. But very often, staff may have been doing their best, so taking the customer's side does not mean penalising staff.

Being the social conscience of your organisation

The leader must set the ethical tone, in terms of behaviour within the organisation and in terms of the organisation's responsibilities to society. This is not a case of laying down moral rules, but through the leader's decisions, people will learn what is and isn't acceptable in the company. Equally, you don't necessarily want to trumpet your ethical standards to the outside world, but people will form a picture of your company from the way it treats customers and staff.

I have a very clear idea of what is acceptable and what isn't. There is always a line we will not cross. We're ruthlessly competitive in the marketplace, but we're honourable about the way we do things. If we tell a supplier the cheque's in the post, it really is in the post.

As the leader, I demonstrate ethical standards in many ways – taking the side of a customer who's been badly treated, but also supporting colleagues if a customer is being unreasonable, helping people who have fallen into hardship, being honest and open with people as far as possible, and putting something back into society through the charitable foundation.

Whom to talk to

Customers and staff aside, as a leader you will be besieged by people wanting your attention. Who do you really need to talk to? The list might be shorter than you think.

The chief deals with many different groups of people: alongside customer and staff, suppliers are an important group. Even though I rarely deal with suppliers direct, I am still there in a figurehead role with them. As with customers, if they are unhappy, I want to know about it.

You will talk regularly to your bankers of course, and your professional advisers such as lawyers, accountants and various specialists in property, IT, distribution and security.

The leader should talk to the press, particularly if there is any bad news. If there is any danger of adverse publicity, it is a mistake to say nothing or hide behind your PR agency. A lot of bad publicity can be forestalled if you are straight with the press, so even though you may hate dealing with the media, they must have a direct line to you so that if something tricky comes up, you know about it immediately. They must be able to get through to you and not be told you're on holiday for two weeks. The only thing worse than having to answer awkward questions from the press, is not answering them and seeing the story all over the next day's papers without your point of view.

Of course I am keen to talk to the press about good news or about anything that will promote my companies but I steer clear of personal profiles. We have had excellent coverage in the broadsheets and specialist press and I love people writing about my business philosophy, but I'm wary of the tabloids because they usually only want the "millionaire in his mansion" kind of story. It can be flattering to be the focus of a personal profile, but you have to think about how it might restrict your freedom. Do you really want people to know about your private life? And what will your people think if you're seen to be getting all the "glory"?

Although the leader should not hide from the press, it is also important to have others in the company dealing with the media. Our group managing director gives many interviews these days and when journalists want to know about the detailed operations of the business, I encourage them to talk to him.

We take the media seriously. Each call from the press has to go through a screening process, so we can be sure it is handled by the right person. If the enquiry is regarding a criticism of the organisation we drop everything to ensure it is dealt with at the highest level.

The other groups of people I talk to are potential new business partners and, of course, my assistants and heads of department.

As my group of businesses has grown, I have had less and less contact with the hi-fi industry.

I don't even deal direct with our banks now. Of course I used to, but for the last five years or so, it has been the group managing director who talks to the banks and handles the company's annual overdraft review.

You might think the bankers would only want to talk to me. But in fact it matters to them that the finances are not all in the hands of one person. They know I'm a grasshopper entrepreneur and I'm always rushing off looking at other business ventures. Our bankers prefer to deal with the managing directors of the various companies in the group, who they know are focused on their own businesses.

There is no doubt the relationship with the bank manager is very important. The relationship is very much with the person, not the bank, because once you have a bank manager who understands your business, that is invaluable. If he or she leaves, you will usually have to start again from scratch with your bank.

David Robinson deals with the manager of the five banks we deal with, and sees them probably once a quarter. It is good to see the bank manager regularly, and perhaps invite him or her to the company's offices so they can get a feel for your business. Rather than only seeing the bank in times of difficulty, when you have to grovel for a bigger overdraft, it is good to develop the relationship when things are going well, so they can understand your strategy for the company.

At the beginning of each month, we send the bank the financial information they require from us. If there are going to be any surprises in the figures, David Robinson rings the bank manager first – so that he realises we're aware of the situation and also to see if we need to talk about it.

I'm not for a moment saying the chair of the company should never deal with the bank manager, but there will come a time when it is right to hand over most of the regular contact to someone else. If bank managers get to deal with half a dozen of my people, and find them competent, that gives them real confidence in the business. So often it's the entrepreneur alone who fronts and 'sells' the business, and the bank wonders if there's anyone else there or if the business would collapse without the chief.

For years and years I wouldn't let go of that kind of contact. But when you're in a strong position, that's the time to hand over. Increasingly, I have first contact with a person - say an important new supplier, or an adviser, and then pass them on to the director who will be dealing with them day to day. Typically I'll hand them over personally to my director and say, "This is one of my right hand people - they'll take care of you. You also have my direct line and my home phone numbers, so if there's ever a problem contact me".

I only do this when I'm confident the director in question will do a good job. Most people I deal with don't mind and perhaps sometimes they are relieved. I'm a bit intense and always in a rush. They prefer to deal with someone who has time for them and can take them to lunch or the occasional social event.

Who inspires the inspirers?

As a leader, you should do a certain amount of hobnobbing with the right people, like heads of other organisations. This kind of networking is stimulating and you learn a lot. It can lead to strategic alliances and valuable non-business initiatives, such as charitable projects.

The more people you network with, the more people will want to know you. I enjoy mixing with bright people, the movers and shakers who get things done. It is very inspiring and you need this when you are surrounded by juniors all day long who are looking to you for inspiration and advice. The person at the top needs to hear good advice and challenging ideas as much as the people lower down the company and the leader is more likely to get this from top people outside the organisation.

When you encounter other leaders you get on with, it is good to meet maybe once or twice a year and talk about the business, or strategy or community service. It never fails to amaze me how many productive ideas can come out of these contacts. You can assist and inspire each other.

Good works

I hate committees, which are nearly always a lot of talk with little outcome. But there are a few key things I have decided I must be involved with.

I don't belong to any trade organisations and loathe industry events. My only involvement with the hi-fi industry is when I go to the "What Hi-Fi?" awards every year, where the industry award winners are announced.

Once you become successful and known as a leader, you do come under pressure to join the great and good. I sit on some charity committees but I'm very selective about which ones and I turn down a lot of requests. If I like the people and they speak my language, I take a view on it. What matters is whether they have enough of a commercial outlook to get any benefit from my input. But I will only be on a committee if I have a say in what happens and my contribution is appreciated and utilised. There is no point in my spending an afternoon listening to other people mouthing off.

My group has its own charitable foundation, which is a very important part of the business because staff and managers from across the group get involved with it. Five per cent of the profits of all the companies in the group go into the charitable foundation.

The foundation itself is run by one manager and an assistant, but she has a large resource of "volunteers" from the rest of the business. Colleagues who are interested can take as much time as they want, within reason, during working hours to get involved with projects. So the company pays for their time, but it is a worthwhile cost - not only because, we hope, the projects do some good, but also because staff enjoy it and it is good for morale.

Like any charitable foundation, we receive requests for funds, which we consider carefully. What we really like to do is to give money, or support in terms of people's time and effort, to original projects. These might be projects we have initiated ourselves, or something undertaken by existing voluntary organisations.

Working on original projects is certainly the most exciting and rewarding kind of involvement. But how do people busy with the rest of their work come up with new and worthwhile ideas?

My old housemaster, Ernest Polack, gave me good advice here. He suggested we focus down on areas we're interested in and research these. This will throw up ideas.

This approach has worked very well. We now have a number of "generic research projects" - GRPs (11 at the time of writing). Groups of staff volunteers get together, headed by someone who is interested in an area to explore, such as projects for the blind or deaf, or spinally injured people. We have projects on animal welfare, human rights and other areas.

The groups meet once a month and the members carry out their own research, for example, talking to blind people and organisations helping them, to discover what kind of support is needed out there. We look for where there are needs we can meet with money or expertise. The spinal injuries group proposed setting up a freephone number for advice on these injuries. We fund the freephone line, but we were also able to use our commercial expertise to negotiate good telephone rates.

Every month, each head of the 11 groups report to the manager of the foundation and the reports are distributed to all the other heads of groups. The heads meet once a month to consider the proposals.

Anyone can have an idea about "doing good", but unless you have proper research, you don't know if the idea has any merit or if other organisations have already implemented it.

I realised this myself when I used to see homeless people on the Embankment being given sandwiches. I thought we could set up a soup kitchen. When I talked to organisations working with the homeless they said there were more than enough soup kitchens to go round. The problem was that people weren't aware of where they were to be found. There was actually an over supply of soup kitchens in some areas but this didn't help kids getting off the train at Kings Cross with nowhere to go. The important thing was getting this information to the people that needed it. So we thought further and came up with the idea for the "On The Right Track" computerised information service now installed in busy locations all over London. This gives free advice on exactly where to go for help if you are homeless or hungry.

It is valuable to be involved with a cross section of activities, apart from your business. There is a difference between writing out a cheque for a charity and actually going and doing something. You can get a lot of benefit from involvement in charities, because they broaden your outlook.

So if an activity is important to you, you'll find the time for it. There is no-one, however big or important they are, who can't find time if they really want to do something. It is a question of prioritising, organising and delegating. One of my favourite sayings is: "If you want something done, give it to a busy person!"

Chapter 11

At the centre of the spider's web

Leading an organisation is like flying an aeroplane. Pilots rely on information and they have dozens of instruments to tell them what they need to know - height, speed, fuel levels. Keeping an eye on all these indicators is not easy, so the cockpit is specially designed for the pilot's convenience, with everything there at a glance.

In the same way, the person at the top of an organisation needs information coming in all the time about the state of the business. The leader can't be everywhere at once, checking on turnover, profits, stock levels, cash flow and so on. So the chief should have management systems specially designed for convenience and economy of effort, feeding back crucial information regularly and accurately.

The leader needs this information in order to make decisions and also as an early warning system if the business is heading for disaster.

The key is to know what information is essential, so that you are not deluged with a flood of trivial facts and reams of computer print-out. Only see the figures you really need to see. But these should cover the whole range of your organisation's activities.

I find it interesting to read about military campaigns, and military leaders rely on good intelligence. A General wants to know the layout of the land, the position and state of the enemy. In battle this has frequently meant the difference between victory and defeat.

Managing the managers

As leader, you are the ultimate manager, the manager's manager. So you need to know how all the different elements of your business are performing - accounts, marketing, distribution, the branches or profit centres, the administrative support. You need to create a web of information systems, with you at the centre like the spider.

It's no good waiting for people to come to your office with news of how well, or badly, they have done. The point is to have data (including bad news) coming back to you automatically and from all directions, so that you are not having to dash around trying to get answers as and when a question comes up.

The web has to be robust and comprehensive. Nothing must be missed, or you will be making decisions based on incomplete data. If information is being fed back regularly, it means an under-performing area cannot store up trouble by hiding their bad figures for weeks on end.

So, what information do you need?

You need to know about your staff. If you believe staff are your most important asset, you should look at all your indicators that show morale and motivation levels - labour turnover, absenteeism and so on. You need constant information and feedback on the state of your troops - how many are fighting fit, how many are about to rebel (none, you hope!), how many are off sick?

Financial review

Financial information is obviously vital. You must keep an eye on the profit and loss, and also on the cash. I know from experience that it is a mistake to lose sight of cashflow. Cash is the fuel that drives the engines of a business and the most profitable company in the world can go bust through lack of cash. It is no good being profitable on paper if you haven't got money when you need it to pay your bills.

A crucially important meeting in any business is the financial review meeting. My group board holds a short, very focused meeting every month when we examine the financial health of the company. Our financial review is effectively our group board meeting. We can achieve a complete review of the business in an hour and a half, concentrating on the figures but of course ranging more widely over business strategy.

Every business, however small, should have a monthly financial review meeting. When you are starting out, it might be be just you and your bookkeeper or outside auditors.

Most of the time you are dealing with all the day to day hassle of running the business. The financial review meeting is completely different: it is your chance to step back and look at the overall picture. You could be working your guts out, but if the company is losing money and moving towards disaster, all your work could be wasted. You need to know in which direction your company is heading.

Another benefit of meeting monthly is that the figures have to be ready for the meeting, to give a financial snapshot of the company. It is a good discipline for yourself or your accounts department to prepare the figures regularly and on time. A common characteristic of a struggling organisation is that its accounts are never complete or up to date. If we have a company within my group which is in trouble, we put it in "intensive care". One of the things its managing director must do on a regular basis is come along to the group board and deliver, in person, a formal report on the figures. He or she has to explain why the figures are bad, or are not ready, which certainly concentrates their mind.

The financial review agenda would include:

Strategy - are we happy with it, does it need shifting?

Capital expenditure - the amount of capital expenditure available for a private company rules how fast it can grow. We do a cap ex projection, identify how to finance it and then monitor how spending matches up against the projection. Capital expenditure will always be needed, for example to fit out new shops, but it eats into your liquidity. It must be controlled so that capital expenditure is not due to exceed a prudent estimate of the profits.

Profit and loss - we look at profit margin, overheads, cash profit, and then the overall picture for each business.

Security - this should be part of your financial review. It can be helpful to start by getting outside consultants to check your security procedures.

Cashflow - we do a cashflow projection 13 weeks ahead. You need to do a "worst" view, which will always look disastrous! Be prudent on sales and assume all deliveries arrive on time. Then take a realistic view of your forthcoming cashflow.

Every six months all the managing directors in the group come up for a day to my house in Yorkshire. They each make a presentation on their company's progress to all the other MDs and myself. This is a very beneficial exercise, from the point of view of both morale and communications.

For a start, it enables the MDs - who otherwise would rarely meet - to get together and talk. This is a useful bonding exercise and strengthens the feeling for them that they are part of a group of companies and are not just on their own. Although the companies are different, the MDs find the problems they encounter can be very similar and so they can learn from each other. Someone else might have had the same difficulty and found a solution; or someone from a different business may suggest a completely new approach. At the same time, I get a rounded picture of how the group is doing and where any weak points might be.

This would be a useful exercise for any organisation. Our MDs find that making the presentation forces them to step back a little and take an objective look at their business and its good and bad points.

Leaders can be very isolated, particularly if their business is still small. On your own, problems can seem completely insoluble, when a detached and sympathetic adviser might be able to suggest a solution straight away. It is worth seeking out advisers like this - someone you can talk to and bounce ideas off. When my business was smaller and we had less experience within the organisation, we used to talk to a consultant. It helps to find someone whose judgment you trust, who will listen and can both challenge and assist you.

A few weeks after these twice-yearly MDs' meetings, the group board will sit down, pull together all the reports from the companies and consider the group's strategic direction. We do not necessarily change the strategy every six months: there may be no need, particularly if the monthly financial review meetings have been working well and the strategy has been successfully tweaked and adapted as we go along.

Knowing the marketplace

When you start out with your own business, you are usually well in touch with what's happening in your marketplace. You are in regular contact with your customers and your suppliers, you know what customers are looking for, what price they are prepared to pay and where else they might go if they are not buying from you.

But as your business grows and you move from behind the counter to an office at the back, from there to a larger office and finally to a glossy headquarters building, it is easy to lose that essential understanding of your customers and the marketplace. To maintain it, you need to have quality market intelligence flowing to you.

You need to know what the competition's doing. At Richer Sounds we refuse to be beaten on price and we look in the high street and in the press to check our rivals' prices. We also use some clever benchmarks. We have found reliable indicators of audio sales throughout the country, which is a gauge of what the public is spending on hi-fi equipment. If audio sales are up, say, 9% one week and our shops' sales figures were up 35%, I know we're whipping the competition. If we seem to be dropping below the national average, I start asking what's wrong.

Staying in touch with customers

This is crucial for the leader of any organisation. If you no longer know what customers want, the whole business will eventually lose touch and lose its sense of direction.

A good leader should be interested in the organisation's customers. You should care about what they want and how best your business can meet their demands. As the business grows, a big danger is that the link with the customer will be broken – and it happens very easily. Even if you just have one shop, as soon as you stop doing the selling yourself and move to the office upstairs, you might as well be a million miles away from your staff and customers. As soon as you move to two shops and so plunge into the issue of employing managers for your business, instead of doing everything yourself, you can get more and more wrapped up in management and move further and further away from your customers. Going from one to two shops is probably the biggest change a company experiences.

That is why I have set up systems that give customers so many opportunities to tell me their demands – even if it is a complaint – and why it is my name on the form for people to write to. I want us to have a dialogue with our customers. We measure and analyse all the customer feedback we get, letters, questionnaires and phone calls.

Of course the people who know most about customers are the people who talk to them – our sales staff. So again we have communication systems for shops to report back on what is happening out there. You can tell a lot from sales figures, but they do not show the whole story.

Where to drill down

From some areas of your business, you will need more detailed information than from others. What these are depends on your business. In retail, for instance, key aspects are buying and marketing: to succeed, you must, first of all buy at the right price, and secondly, sell with a satisfactory profit margin.

You might want to keep a closer eye on areas where your top managers have weak points, so that you can prop them up a bit and spot any problems before they take hold. But, for example, if your property manager is fantastic at delivering the deals you want, you won't need to spend much time on that and can leave them to get on with it. You are spinning all these plates on sticks, and there will always be some sticks that need an extra twirl.

The top person in any business should be wisest and the best informed. To be a genuine leader, and not merely a top manager, you should know the business inside out.

For me, that means being fully in touch with buying and marketing. It does not mean making all the buying and marketing decisions myself. Buying decisions are crucial, but there is always the danger of one person taking a narrow view, of being over enthusiastic about certain products and not understanding others, of getting carried away after a jolly lunch with suppliers.

To get round this, we have a buying group, which has to approve all the buying decisions. At least half of the 12 people in the group are from the shop floor. They are in touch with how popular certain products are, what problems arise, what people are asking for, what is selling or not. They bring the buying down to earth. We stipulate that no buying decisions can be made by one person alone, because it is less easy to be swayed if there are two of you. For the same reason, we hold buying meetings at 8 o'clock in the morning, when you look at everything with a cool and sceptical eye.

I usually attend buying group meetings. I want to know who's doing the deals, who's got what products, what should we be stocking, what new things are coming along.

My real role in the buying group is to push people. It worries me if I hear a chief executive say, "I've got a great buying team – I just let them get on with it". Part of our mission is always to give the customer better value for money, so I am always driving my people to get better deals. I'm there to ask, "Was that the best deal we could get? Could we have done it differently?"

The information flow

Every evening I receive the sales figures and the cash profit by branch, which are prepared manually. It is important to recognise there are two types of management information: the estimates and then proving the estimates.

So on a Sunday morning, when I look at information on how we've done up to Saturday night, I am looking at estimates. Our system is excellent: I get a grid of detailed information, branch by branch, faxed over to me. Sales can be known exactly, but the cash profit each day has to be estimated. In a retail business you know how much you have taken and can approximately judge what the margin is, and therefore the profit, but you cannot know how much you have really made until you count your stock at the end of a trading period. The real margin will have to reflect any shrinkage. It's no good saying "we sold 10 of these and made £10 profit each, that's £100 profit" if you later discover you had something nicked out of the back door worth £50, so you have really only made £50.

We do a stock-take every two months, which is frequent. Many businesses only stock-take once a year – so they only truly know how well they are doing once a year. You need both types of information: your approximate figure as quickly as possible, in order that you can react accordingly; and a more accurate figure to prove your estimate later on.

Too many inexperienced businesses get this wrong. One of our new companies initially told me they were making 24% gross profit on sales. When we did their accounts after several months their margin actually came out at 16% – a disastrous discrepancy. We then had to find out what had gone so wrong. Was it a mistake in the accounts, a mistake in counting the stock or a serious problem with theft? It is better to find out after four months than after a year of trading.

So the leader's job is not only to receive information, but also to question it critically.

Clearly you have to keep track of all this information. I get about 30 different reports at the end of each week, so I tick them off against a checklist on a Sunday night and chase up the ones I haven't received on Monday morning. As well as reports from the divisional directors, there will be things like the analysis of calls to our freephone number, our group cash flow forecast, sales analysis, distribution figures, and so on.

You also have to keep track of information when you act on it. I devised a grid of information for use when making calls to the branches. I used to make these calls myself, but now they are done by the group MD or deputy MD on a Monday morning, to the same organised format. The grid shows exactly what each branch has been doing and the matters needed to be raised with them.

The point is that we don't ring up a branch and say, "did you have a good week last week?" We already know whether they did or not and are ready to congratulate them if they did, and find out what the problem is if they didn't. People will lose respect for their chief if they realise he or she hasn't got a clue what they are doing.

I thrive on information. I have two takings books, one month to view – one for Richer Sounds and one for the other businesses. They show takings figures and cash profits.

I have another blue book where I write down all the other things we measure. This shows items such as deliveries in, the amount of warranties we sell, the conversion rate and the commission we pay, stock turnover, the number of responses on our 0500 number, the rate of repair turnaround, the out of stock figures and many more.

It does not take long to do: I fill in a few lines per week. But it is a goldmine of information and allows me to make quick comparisons month by month and year by year.

Leaders must have at their fingertips the data to be able to make decisions. In isolation, many of these figures look too detailed to be meaningful, and perhaps relatively trivial. But they build up into an informed and three-dimensional picture of how your organisation is doing.

Some of the new MDs we appoint in the group are not confident about financial matters when they start out. We give them training and impress on them how important it is to understand the figures. Once they realise you don't need a degree in economics to understand financial accounting, they have a much better grip on their business.

Leaders don't need to be accountants themselves. But they need the ability to ask educated and sensible questions about the accounts. They must be capable of looking at a sheet of figures submitted by the accountants and immediately seeing any glaring errors, preferably without using a calculator.

Each of our MDs has an end of month checklist to ensure that all the financial and operational reports have been completed. The leader should never say, "Oh I leave all that to my finance director". You have to take responsibility for the finances: if things go wrong, it is no use blaming the accountants. This is particularly true in a small company that uses an external bookkeeper. The chances are the bookkeeper will have other clients and will not remember when you need priority information. The leader must be the one demanding that information.

Of course you must not get bogged down in detail and fail to see the wood for the trees. You have to keep your vision of where the business is going and your long-term strategy, as your plan of how to get there. But it is facts and figures that will show you whether you are achieving your strategy or veering off course. They are an early warning system indicating problems, whether in the finances, customer service or in management and staff morale. Good information puts you in charge, which is where the leader ought to be.

Chapter 12

Ten steps to great leadership

1. Take an honest look at yourself.

The first step to being a great leader is to assess how good a leader you are now. The most important judges of your leadership are your own managers and workforce. No matter how great you think you are, if you are not inspiring your own people, you are not an effective leader.

Of course, you cannot ask your employees direct. If you go round asking, "Am I a good boss?", it would be a brave person who said "no".

You do not need to know about your popularity. Being a good leader is not about being liked. What you want to know is whether people feel inspired, part of a team that knows where it is going, whether they grasp your vision for the organisation and understand the strategy for achieving that vision.

You also need to know what they think of your leadership skills. Do they find you are a good decision maker? Do people feel they are given enough information or do they think you keep them in the dark? Do they have confidence that you will do what you say you will do? Do your managers believe that you delegate enough to them and allow them to get on with their job?

Many of these are subjective perceptions, but important. You might think you are an excellent communicator, but if people are always complaining behind your back that "nobody ever tells us anything!" – you are doing something wrong.

An employee attitude survey is an excellent way to discover what people think of your leadership skills and, more importantly, to assess whether you are improving. In my business, we carry out a survey annually. Every employee is asked to fill in a form with a range of questions. They do not have to give their name and the questionnaires are processed in the utmost confidence, by a member of staff who is not a senior manager, so people know they can be completely honest without fear of recrimination from their boss.

The value of a survey is, not so much in the answers to the questions, but how it shows changes over time. If one year, 50% of people say they agree with the statement "I enjoy my job" and the next year it is 65%, the leader can know that things are going right and that, perhaps, recent initiatives to make work more fun are having an effect. If the figure nosedives to 35% the following year, urgent action is needed.

A number of questions relate to leadership. It might be an idea to make a leadership matrix, pulling out the five most relevant questions that reflect on leadership and seeing how attitudes change. These might be questions on statements like "I am kept well informed of what is going on in the company" or "When we have a problem, the top management of the company are sympathetic and keen to help".

Remember, the questions may not refer to you personally, because the majority of the workforce will probably not be working directly with you. But the responses to statements like "I am proud to be working for the company", reflect directly on your performance as a leader.

The other important way to assess how well you are doing now is, of course, to look at the performance of the organisation. Effective leaders provide better returns than their peers in the same industry.

Commercial companies will be constantly measuring indicators such as sector averages, returns on investment, margins, growth rate, market share, profits and earnings per share. Non-commercial organisations are increasingly able to measure their performance too, through league tables and other indicators.

Again, the key task is to measure change. This book tells you how to improve as a leader and the results should eventually show through in the performance of your organisation.

2. Examine your social conscience

If you are on your way to being a great leader in the eyes of your workforce, and of your bank manager or shareholders, what about in the eyes of society?

Having a social conscience is one of the things that distinguishes a great leader from the average chief executive.

Part of it is good business sense. It pays to take good care of your employees. If you are honest with them and do not cheat or exploit them, they are far more likely to be honest with you and not steal from the business. They are also more likely to treat customers in an honest and fair way and good customer service is good for business. A culture of integrity and fairness is motivating: people feel confident they will be rewarded for a good job and that they will be protected if they speak out against lies, theft or harassment. That integrity and fairness will also be displayed in the organisation's dealings with the outside world, not only with customers but also with suppliers. There is a contribution to the wider business community if suppliers are treated properly, paid on time and so on.

The leader is the role model here. It is important to have a social conscience because the leader has a great deal of power to influence everyone else in the company, so with that power must come responsibility.

If you are a strong leader, people model themselves on you, and your model must be one of integrity. You don't have to be a saint. What people do at home is their own business, but within the workplace, there has to be trust between colleagues.

I believe businesses put a great deal into society, principally by providing good quality jobs and also through the taxes they pay. I stress "good quality", because poorly paid, insecure jobs are doing nothing for society and give the business sector a bad name.

I also put more in, via the 5% of our profits which go into our charity foundation. As a business, we don't need to do this: plenty of companies give nothing to charity. But we enjoy doing it and we hope it has given rise to some valuable projects. Being a good leader and not just a boss is often about the extra things you choose to do.

3. Be organised, be reliable...

Being organised won't in itself make you a great leader (though it might make you a great filing clerk). But there's no escaping the fact that you can't be a great leader without being organised.

Read chapter 5 and use all the tools at your disposal to order your working time. You have to get organised if you are to deliver what you have promised to do. Your staff must be able to rely on you.

Great leaders get the work done, meet deadlines, make decisions and have a clear desk at the end of the day. It sounds dull – but in fact it's another element that marks out the great leaders from the average. Great leaders are immensely productive. That isn't necessarily because they have more energy or work longer hours than anyone else. It can be because they are better organised and get the maximum out of each working day.

4. ...then let go.

You are only an effective leader if you know how to delegate. Doing everything yourself is not leadership.

Once you delegate, you can do more and more. Then your business can grow and you can lead your organisation on to great things. With layers of 10 - you delegate to 10 key people around you and they each manage another 10 and so on - you can effectively lead a workforce of thousands.

Delegating does not mean giving up power and responsibility. On the contrary - it is hard work because to delegate effectively you have to manage your key people, set them clear tasks and deadlines, then follow up and monitor the results. You must have the systems in place for information to be fed back to you. Once again, you have to be organised.

Letting go is difficult. It looks risky at first and requires courage. To delegate effectively, there is a balance that constantly needs to be achieved between letting people get on with the jobs you have given them, and maintaining control. It is not easy, but getting the balance right is the way to great leadership.

5. Develop your team

A leader can be judged on the quality of his or her team of senior managers. When people praise one of my top team, I'm really proud because it reflects on me.

These are the people you delegate to and who see that your ideas and decisions are cascaded down the organisation, so they must be good. Their performance is a reflection of the quality of leadership in a number of ways. Firstly, they are an indication of the leader's skills in judging the right person for the job. Secondly, a good leader will attract and retain good managers. Intelligent and dynamic people will quickly tire of working for a weak leader.

Thirdly, it is the leader's responsibility to develop his or her key people. You must coach them, train them, push them to learn and go further, so that the whole organisation can go forward.

If you have surrounded yourself with safe, unadventurous yes-men, that is a sign of poor leadership. Your key people do not have to be replicas of you (much better if they are not!) but they must be committed to your vision and your drive to push the organisation forward.

6. Bravery under pressure

Times of crisis are often a true test of leadership. Great leaders are the ones who do not let their people down in difficult periods. They do not lie to the workforce about the situation or require employees to take pay-cuts they would never dream of taking themselves.

Great leaders are the ones who lead from the front. They do not hide behind the public relations people when it comes to announcing bad news, or leave town while the human resources director has the terrible job of announcing redundancies.

Great leaders take the pain and the blame. But they are also the ones who can inspire their people to rally round in hard times and pull the organisation out of its difficulties.

7. Communicate

Good communication is an essential part of leadership. This does not mean the leader has to be a superb conference speaker or a witty raconteur - it is more to do with having effective lines of communication open throughout the organisation. The communication should be two-way: great leaders listen as well as talk.

You cannot lead people unless you communicate with them. You must inspire people with your vision for the organisation, as well as giving the orders to put that vision into practice. A chat from the chairman once a year is not enough: people need to be kept informed regularly of what is happening if they are to feel involved in the company.

Effective communication also means checking that the message has got through. I make a video each month for the staff, which is a great way of sending a personal message about what is going on. But I don't like talking to myself, so I check up on whether every branch has watched the video.

A key difference between great leaders and the average boss is that great leaders encourage upwards communication.

To be a great leader, you must be ready to listen to staff, and to act on what you hear. A great leader is never too busy to find time in the diary for a 10 minute talk with a member of staff. Listening also means putting in systems of upwards communication, so that people always have a recognised outlet, either for their complaints or their bright ideas. It is also important to let people know when complaints have been dealt with, or ideas implemented, or else people will feel they have been talking to a brick wall.

The leader must listen to customers and suppliers. However big the organisation, a good leader will be in touch with what customers want. Good customer service is not just a matter for the sales assistant: it is also the leader's responsibility. The leader is also a figurehead for suppliers, recognising that they play an important part in the success of the business.

8. Learn from your mistakes.

Until leaders admit that they make mistakes, they cannot be truly effective. Great leaders are not the paragons who never make mistakes, but the ones who make mistakes and learn from them.

Great leaders might make a lot of mistakes, because they take risks and try new things. But they treat failures as an opportunity to analyse what went wrong, how that can be avoided in future, and then to apply that lesson so that the rest of the business is strengthened as a result.

One of the most important steps on the way to being a great leader is to ensure that you learn every day. This does not always mean learning from mistakes - successes have a lot to teach as well. It is as vital to know what you've done right as to know what you've done wrong. The key is to admit to yourself that, however many years you've been in business, you don't know everything and you can always learn and improve. Arrogance is a barrier to great leadership.

9. Generate continuous improvement

In the same way as you personally learn and improve, your organisation must be constantly improving. A great leader has the drive and the ability to generate this kai zen, or continuous improvement.

It is easy for even a successful organisation to get stuck in a rut, always doing things the same way because no-one has bothered to look for a better way. To get out of this rut requires drive and energy, the ability to question and challenge accepted practices and a restless desire to find a better way. Great leaders are never satisfied: they always want to see things improved.

The mark of great leadership is to have this search for improvement permeating the entire organisation. The leader must also organise and control this search. A business buzzing with ideas is not enough: there must be an effective suggestion scheme so that ideas are channelled through to senior management. The ideas must be recognised and rewarded. If they are put into practice there must be a consistent approach, so that improvements are made throughout the company. If there is a better way, everyone should be doing it that way.

10. Have a life

Being a great leader means getting some kind of balance into your life. Most chiefs work hard - the trick is to work smarter, not harder. A good step to great leadership might be to take some time off and remind your family what you look like.

The leader will almost always be under a lot of pressure and to lead the organisation well, he or she needs to stay fit and sane. You won't benefit your business if you drive yourself to an early heart attack. Nor will you make good decisions if you are so stressed out, you can't think straight.

Stress is part of the leader's day. My four tips for dealing with it are: talk to people; take gentle, regular exercise; be determined; and be organised.

Exercise, a healthy diet, avoiding dependence on cigarettes or alcohol are not trivial issues: you owe it to yourself and the organisation to be on top form.

They are also an indicator. If your immediate reaction is, "I never have time for exercise", you are not being an effective leader. Something is wrong if you can't spare 20 minutes twice a week for a brisk walk. Something is equally wrong if you work 'til 10pm every night and haven't taken a holiday in five years. You are not delegating enough, or you are not managing your time properly.

Perhaps you think you just live for your work, especially if it is your own business, your baby - but great leaders have broad interests. They look beyond the four walls of their office. They get ideas from unexpected quarters, from other industries or other countries. They are in touch with the outside world, which means in the end they are more in touch with the customers and can stay one step ahead of the competition.

You might be thinking, "It's easy for him to say "take a day off" but I can't do that!" But I'm speaking from actual experience here. I really do run a group of companies, remain thoroughly in control, and also have the time to take holidays, go out with mates, spend the weekend in Yorkshire and walk my dogs. I also have the time to do work for a number of charities, advise some very large companies and explore new business opportunities. It can be done, if you delegate and organise yourself.

I don't claim to be a great leader. But I aspire to it and I'm learning all the time. I believe I do know what it takes to be an effective leader and I also believe very many chiefs could become better leaders, particularly if they started to listen to their people.

"If things went brilliantly - you did it"
"If things went well - we did it"
"If things went badly - I did it"
General George S. Patton 1885 - 1945